5·3·76

All Silver and No Brass

At Christmastime in Ulster, not so long ago, young men wearing colored tunics and tall pointed hats that covered their faces used to go from house to house presenting a play for their neighbors. They enacted a short rhymed drama in which Saint Patrick was killed and miraculously resurrected, collected money for the Mummers' Ball—hoping for "all silver and no brass"—and departed to the sound of flute or tin whistle. Irish Christmas mumming, the subject of this carefully researched and beautifully written book, is approached in Part I through the haunting and poetic recollections of four old people of the hamlet of Ballymenone who recall the mumming from their youth. Through many hours of conversation with the author, they recollect the celebration of the "Great Days" of the seasonal cycle, recite verses from the plays, and relive the emotions of Christmases past.

In Part II, "Rhyme and Reason," the author examines the form and function of the mummers' play, showing that —contrary to the theories of some folkorists—it is not a truncated fragment of a much larger whole but a complete "presentational" statement.

(continued on back flap)

(continued from front flap)

He shows how the mummers' play functioned, not as a purposeless survival, but as a means of drawing the community closer together and as an expression of dangers and hopes in the potentially bitter Ulster situation. Taken in its totality, mumming was an art, a powerfully compacted expression of a traditional aesthetic and of a system of values that endured for centuries and has only recently failed.

Most of the scholarship on the folk drama of Britain and Ireland has consisted of speculation about origins founded upon naked texts of plays. Glassie's study is a departure from this pattern because it treats fully the social and cultural context of the mummers' play. In Part III of the book Glassie returns to the four old people of Ballymenone who were his informants, draws loving portraits of them, and describes his often moving experiences while collecting material. This is a superb study, of obvious value to folklorists, but also of interest to literary critics, literary historians, anthropologists, and others.

AN IRISH CHRISTMAS MUMMING

All Silver and No Brass

HENRY GLASSIE

Illustrated by the Author

INDIANA UNIVERSITY PRESS

Bloomington & London

Published in Canada by Fitzhenry & Whiteside Limited,
Don Mills, Ontario

Manufactured in the United States of America

Designed by Guy Fleming

Library of Congress Cataloging in Publication Data

Glassie, Henry H
All silver and no brass.

Bibliography
Includes index.
1. Folk drama, Irish—History and criticism.
2. Mumming plays. I. Title.
PR8793.F6G6   398.2'36   75-9132
ISBN 0-253-30470-9   1 2 3 4 5 79 78 77 76 75

For my mother and my grandmother

Mumm me moe mummers!

— Finnegans Wake

CONTENTS

Bright Waters, Green Isle: A Preface   *xi*

Acknowledgments   *xxi*

Four Conversations

Ellen Cutler: *I Loved to See the Mummers Come*   *3*

Hugh Nolan: *I'll Tell You the Way It Was*   *11*

Peter and Joseph Flanagan: *A Little Entertainment*   *20*

Michael Boyle: *We Used to Mum in Our Country*   *38*

Rhyme and Reason

Survival: *The Ould Customary Thing*   *53*

Geography: *A Custom in These Islands*   *68*

Performance: *Go in with a Vengeance*   *76*

Meaning: *The Performance of the Season*   *91*

Function: *To Bring Unity amongst Them*   *122*

Envoi

Fare Thee Well for a While   *145*

Glossary   *153*

Bibliography   *162*

Notes   *170*

Index   *189*

Illustrations

PLATES (following page xxiv)

Joseph and Peter Flanagan
The land
The Arney River
A forth across the bog
Lough Erne and Inishmore from Ballymenone
The view from Mrs. Cutler's
Mrs. Cutler's
Mrs. Cutler and her son John
Rooking hay
The Twelfth of July in Enniskillen
The Arney River

DRAWINGS IN TEXT

Map of County Fermanagh in Ireland	*xiii*
Map of Ballymenone in southern County Fermanagh	*xiv*
Here comes I	*6*
He gives Saint Patrick a stab of it	*15*
He'll slap down on the floor	*30*
All silver and no brass	*46*
Them was the mummers	*47*
It's very easy makin a mummer's hat	*81*
Plan of the play as integrating action	*89*
The Ballymenone year	*96*
St. Brighid's cross	*111*
The conquest of death	*120*
Doin the town	*141*
Besom and creepie at the Flanagans' hearth	*154*
Fadge in the oven at Mrs. Cutler's hearth	*156*
The south Fermanagh spade	*160*

Bright Waters, Green Isle:

A PREFACE

W INTER NIGHTS IN IRELAND are black and long. A sharp
wet wind often rises through them. Midwinter is a time
to sit by the fire, safe in the family's circle, waiting for the
days to lengthen and warm. It is no time for venturing out
into cold darkness. The ground is hard, the winds bitter. But
for two and a half centuries, and possibly for many years beyond them, young men braved the chilly lanes, rambling as
mummers from house to house, brightening country kitchens
at Christmas with a comical drama. Their play, compact, poet-
ical, and musical, introduced an antic crew and carried one
character through death and resurrection.

Mumming has long intrigued literary scholars who imagine
the play, so common in nineteenth century England and Scotland as well as Ireland, to be a lost wanderer from the Middle
Ages. Conceivably, they dream, it attended at the mysterious
birth of the European dramatic arts.

I met the mummers first in a book that was recommended
in a fine course on medieval drama I took as an undergraduate.
In those days my spare time was spent badgering old people
along the North Carolina Blue Ridge to sing ballads into my
tape-recorder. My interest was immediate. The stark intensity
of the mummers' rhymes reminded me of the ballads. Although
my main interests drifted elsewhere, I kept up with the scholarship on mumming and was delighted with the publication of
Alan Gailey's *Irish Folk Drama*.

In 1972 the John Simon Guggenheim Memorial Foundation
awarded me a generous fellowship so that I could take time

away from teaching in Indiana University's Folklore Institute to do some field research in Ireland. Before my family and I left home, it occurred to me that I might be able to talk with some men who had been mummers. The older scholars had not asked the questions that interested me. They had studied texts of the plays but had largely ignored the players. They had used the texts as prods to speculation about the early history of drama and ritual, but they had paid little attention to the play as performance, as the embodiment of intention, the vehicle for meaning. Their probings had been too shallow and narrow. They had not given the play or its people their due.

Mumming was neither my project nor my goal. My project was the creation of an existentially grounded ethnography of people in trouble. Most ethnographers have sought stable situations that can be reduced to static models, but I was interested in trying to understand how real people endure moments of violent change. The Irish border country seemed a good choice. My goal was involvement with others. The philosopher may be able to answer his questions introspectively, but the folklorist (or the anthropologist or the historian) comes to his comprehension of self through engaged and compassionate comparison with other people. I thought that the persistent, resilient people of the south Ulster hills would be able to help me. I was right.

We settled next to the barbed-wire bound barracks in the southwest Ulster town of Enniskillen, in the County Fermanagh, about twelve miles north and east of the burning border. I began quickly, luxuriously conducting my study on foot. I came to know every dog, bog, path and field in a small area south of the town, lying west of Upper Lough Erne, its waters as bright, its isles as green as promised in the old ballad of the Inniskilling Dragoon.

I walked, wandering at first to find some natural social limits on a landscape that carried no obvious physical community, for I wished to pass the time I had among people who interacted regularly with one another. It was not long before I had marked out a wobbly rectangle, measuring about three by

Map of County Fermanagh in Ireland

one and a half miles, that was known informally as the Lower End of the Parish. Its southern border was the little Arney River. Its northern boundary ran west from the silvery Lough to the Bellanaleck Cross, with its store, tilting gray church (Church of Ireland), and hall for the Loyal Orange Lodge— west from Bellanaleck, past the chapel (Catholic) to the Arney Cross, with its store and pair of public houses.

Looking over the land, its many hills seem small, but when you walk it over, it rises and falls constantly, abruptly. Thinking about the little hills increases their size, for small differences

Map of Ballymenone in southern County Fermanagh

in elevation mean large differences in ecology. The low areas dipping between the hills are filled with bog where turf is cut to keep a fire on the hearth. Around the bog's edge lies the moss ground where gardens are planted, and above that rises the clay upland which was once cultivated but is hedged now into meadows and pastures. Along the grain of the hillsides, the houses are set, the old ones of stone or local brick, the newer ones of cement block, most of them whitewashed until they shine, a few still snug under gold thatch covers. Often at the hill's top stands a perfect circle of trees, rooted in the earthworks of an Iron Age homestead. Some say these "forths" are now the habitations of fairies, others are skeptical, but few are willing to disturb the trees that grow or the limbs that fall there. Above the hills spread the ever varying, usually rainladen skies.

Most of the kitchens at the centers of those white houses were opened willingly, generously to me. Like any fieldworker who is serious about what he is doing, I got to know only a few people very well, but I had nice chats with a great many people, drank vast quantities of tea, and got a good feeling for demographic generalities. A few people who live there have jobs out of the area, but for most their homes and work are one. It remains a thoroughly agricultural—or, more exactly, a horticultural and pastoral place. Most fortunes, large or small, come from the sale of cattle that graze over the low drumlins. It has been two generations since Irish was spoken there, so my language was sufficient to the delicate interests I nurtured. My Americanness set me outside the local social categories, so I got on well with people of opposed political and religious persuasions. More of the people were Catholics than Protestants, more were men than women, more were old than young. Almost all had made courageous adaptations within the terrors that frame our lives.

That was what interested me most: how daily life passed sanely, even artfully, despite armored cars hurtling down the country lanes, despite bombs that cracked the air and rattled the windows. I had forgotten all about mumming. Then one evening Mrs. Cutler and I were chatting about Christmas and she mentioned the mummers' arrival as the season's highpoint. Suddenly excited, I asked if any of the play's performers were still alive, and she listed people I knew well. All of them were men in their sixties and seventies who had begun to stand out in my thinking as exceptionally energetic, outgoing, and articulate. From that time on, I asked many questions about the drama, its performance, meaning, and purpose. I learned that the memory of mumming is cherished and that my suspicion that the older scholars had misled us about the drama's nature was correct.

Bright Waters, Green Isle: A Preface

This book's first part consists of four conversations I had with people about mumming. I present them to you as they happened. They were tape-recorded and in transcribing the recordings I made no changes in the play's text or any of the anecdotes and kept other editing to a minimum: I rearranged a bit, but left nothing out except a few of my own comments. The words are all theirs. I worked to let the transcriptions represent their cadences and emphases accurately, and I have added a glossary to this book's end to help you enter their semantic. Had I beaten these conversations into a single statement, the realities that theories are designed to explain would have been obscured, and the human beings who actually know about mumming would have been eliminated.

Social scientists customarily study people as effectively conditioned animals or as passive carriers of a closed, inert abstraction called culture. But the ideas of real people are developed in a quirky and open, continuous dialectic of the shared and the personal. These separate conversations reveal individual styles as well as cultural data. They display the variability without which culture could not change and a person could not exist happily.

The conversations provide us our text, but the play is easily misunderstood and difficult to appreciate, as much of the scholarship on mumming unintentionally proves. So, this book needs its second part which consists of the reports of other conversations, some glossing and theorizing.

As is the case with all disciplines built around the study of man, folklore has its humanists and its social scientists. R. J. E. Tiddy began the first book on mumming, *The Mummers' Play*, by commenting that studies of folk literature seem to belong equally to literary historians and anthropologists. Since his time, movements have gathered within folklore in an attempt to purify our study in imitation of some social or behavioral science. These movements have benefited the discipline, but they have not been completely successful. In general, I have been in sympathy with such scientizing efforts, for our study is too important to do casually, but I feel now that much of folklore's tensile strength comes from bridging the academic boundary which separates the rigorous but sometimes trivial sciences from the profound but often vague humanities. The theoretical tradition that aided me most during the composition of this book's second part is social scientific, but what I wished to accomplish is the same thing that any critic does with a work of art he takes seriously.

I walked the Irish hills, green in all seasons, and passed long nights by the turf fires to experience the world and learn how to act against it, and I wrote this book to discover new dimensions in the phenomena I chose to contemplate. But why do I set it, text and analysis, before you?

If you are a folklorist fascinated by mumming, no problem arises. Here are new data, new thoughts—a contribution.

If you are not a mumming enthusiast, one reason I offer this to you can be taken from a fact about my discipline. Folklorists converse excitedly about great matters, about the traditional and artistic, the genuine, sincere, and human. But we have been inept in communicating our interests. Our technical writings, insecurely conceived in the shadows of giant scientists, have been smothered under cowardly jargoning. Our popular writings have regularly demeaned our subject, making jokes of jokes and items of art, leaving others wondering why we do what we do. While I wrote this book, one goal I kept in mind is that it should be an honest presentation of how and why one folklorist practices his craft.

In a larger frame, more ideological than professional, I wanted to present the reader with a sensation of complexity. Mumming and mummers, like other arts and peoples contemptuously termed folk or primitive, have been dismissed as simple and banished from serious consideration to ethnology. If the depth and richness of the arts of the world's dark and poor people could be exposed, there would be no argument for colonialism, no comfort in pride. I wrote this book to introduce you to a few people of the sort we customarily ignore while scurrying through our mad routines. I want you to meet and respect them.

The people who told me about mumming lived near one another in the Lower End of the Parish. This comprised five townlands bundled into a district called Ballymenone and six townlands to the west of Ballymenone. The traditional townland divisions are not large, incorporating here from two to fifteen houses. (I will refrain from any mention of townland names in a little effort at privacy, for people's townlands are their addresses.) These people know each other well. The Flanagans have worked for the Cutlers, Hugh Nolan and Michael Boyle were close friends, Peter Flanagan and Michael Boyle were members of the same mumming squad. Though it may not always seem so, they are all describing the same mummers.

I visited Mrs. Cutler, Hugh Nolan, and the Flanagans about twice a week from July through December of 1972, and Michael Boyle about as often from October through December. On each of those days I picked up some bit of information and developed some emotional understanding that helped as I wrote, but my main mumming interviews were: Mrs. Cutler (July 26, August 11), Hugh Nolan (August 23), Peter and Joseph Flanagan (July 3, November 6), Michael Boyle (October 26, November 20).

Once I had transcribed the tapes, scratched out a draft of this book, and found myself with more questions than answers, I luckily got invited to Northern Ireland to consult on a matter of architectural restoration. While 1973 became 1974, I had a week with my friends in Fermanagh and very profitable mumming chats with Hugh Nolan (January 2), and the Flanagans (December 30, January 2). It was then that, tickled by my obsession, P Flanagan teased:

"Aw sure, I'll go over to Indiana sometime. I'll form up a mummin team and go out."

Acknowledgments

ONE OF THE PLEASANTEST PARTS of book writing is offering public thanks to the many who helped the book be.

My first debt is to the John Simon Guggenheim Memorial Foundation for allowing my old dream of an extended stay in Ireland to become a reality. And I am thankful to Eric Montgomery and Bob Oliver for engineering my return in 1973.

My deepest debt is to those who taught me about mumming, my collaborators in this book's content: Michael Boyle, Ellen Cutler, Peter and Joseph Flanagan, Hugh Nolan. They are more than collaborators in name, as I have arranged for all this book's royalties to be divided among them.

There were many other people in southern Fermanagh who helped me learn about their culture and I wish to thank them too: James Boyle, Johnny Boyle, John Carson, Marian Cathcart, Mr. and Mrs. Gabriel Coyle, Martin Crudden, Dick and John Cutler and their families, John Drum, John Gileece, Bob Lambe, Mr. and Mrs. Tommy Love and family, Tommy and P Lunny, William Lunny, John Joe Maguire, Oney McBrien, Mr. and Mrs. Paddy McBrien and family, James McGovern, Rose and Joe Murphy, Mr. and Mrs. John O'Prey, Mr. and Mrs. Hugh Patrick Owens and family, Mrs. James Owens, James and Annie Owens, Mr. and Mrs. Bobbie Thornton. Our time in the town was made enjoyable by Mr. and Mrs. John Hynes, Mr. and Mrs. John McGowan, and George McQuillan.

Ireland's scholars were generous with their time and information, putting us up, guiding me, and opening their rich archives. I am grateful to E. Estyn Evans, George Thompson, and Alan Gailey in Belfast, to Seán Ó Súilleabháin, Caoimhín Ó Danachair, and Bo Almqvist in Dublin.

While this book was forming, my friends—colleagues and students—at Indiana University provided me with an interesting environment, and my university's Press proved a delight to work with. Adam Horvath gave me crucial encouragement, warm fellowship, and a nice pun. Kate Torrey gave the manuscript a gentle, sensitive editing.

My family's help has been constant. My parents and grandmother continue to feign interest in what I do, despite the obscurities of scholastic style; it was partially for them I wrote this book in a comprehensible manner. My wife, Betty-Jo, again typed and typed, and she and Polly, Harry, and Lydia went with me to Fermanagh.

I like thinking of this as our book.

All Silver and No Brass

Joseph and Peter Flanagan

The land

The Arney River

A forth across the bog
Lough Erne and Inishmore from Ballymenone

The view from Mrs. Cutler's

Mrs. Cutler's

Mrs. Cutler and her son John

Rooking hay

The Twelfth of July in Enniskillen

FOUR

CONVERSATIONS

———————

Ellen Cutler

Hugh Nolan

Peter and Joseph Flanagan

Michael Boyle

Ellen Cutler:

I Loved to See the Mummers Come

BEYOND THE ORANGE LILIES, fenced next to the street, and over the low hills, hedged into smooth small fields, the sky pales. It thickens slowly, darkens slowly. No sudden change comes on a long summer's evening: edges soften, forms melt, blues and greens fade.

Mrs. Cutler sits straight on the edge of her big chair at the corner of the hearth. Her hair, never cut, lies plaited down her back. She watches the window's square of sky. You expect to see, nearly hear, the line separating night from day, but twilight abides, relentlessly, night slides in unseen and silent.

She turns from the window and back to our conversation on the Great Days that punctuate the year's circle. The day's last light is trapped in the buffed brass of the front door latch, the knobs on the dresser's drawers. She says:

"Christmas was a great time. Now. A great time all right."

She tongs the sticks of the fire into order. Sticks, she feels, make a cheerier fire than turf, and they are as good as turf for baking fadge, so she keeps a good heap of sticks next to the lane, near where she has tied that bad villain of a goat whose tastes require the paling around the orange lilies. She leans the tongs against the jamb of the hearth. It is painted green with pink dots.

"We went out and got red–berried holly—red berries on the holly. And I used to put that up on the dresser . . . "

Our eyes follow her hand upward past the shelves of delph, gleaming, spiraling across the dresser that stands opposite the kitchen's hearth. She loves to take those plates down, each the memory of some occasion, wash them and set them up again neatly. They are not used; there are plates to eat from in the pantry. She turns, sweeping a gesture over her "ornaments," symmetrically arrayed: china ducks and a plastic Santa on a shelf at the rear, a donkey's shoe over the front door, plates on the wall with verse and Irish scenes, an embroidered Lead Me and Guide Me, an aerial photograph of her farm, a print of a thatched house, another of a dog, calendars.

" . . . and round behind the pictures. Well then, I used to get paper decorations for the ceilin. And balloons. Oh, and things like that, you know.

"That'd be just before Christmas, and then Christmas day would come along, and we'd be watchin for our presents. And children were here, and they used to get alot of things.

"Then, there was always a goose or maybe two goose for the dinner. Big fat dinner. I never eat goose, for I don't like it. Neither I do.

"The men would have a jorum of maybe old porter or whiskey. Well, I could take a half-one of whiskey all right—and maybe two. I don't deny it.

"And the children was playin with their toys, and had a good dinner, and we sat around the fire chattin till it was time to go out and do the work again, milkin and feedin and all like that on a farm. You were always goin. And very little for it.

"But sure we got on."

She pauses, thinking. Some celebrated their Christmas in the Room, the parlor off the kitchen—above the fireplace in most of the old Fermanagh houses like Mrs. Cutler's. An ancient tall clock and dark dining room furniture stand in her Room. The local Orange Lodge met there before the hall was built at Bellanaleck. King Billy equestrian, George V and his queen, Sir Edward Carson, and members of the family are tightly framed on the papered walls. The Room is a piece of sculpture, rarely used. Christmas at the Cutlers' always happened in the kitchen; it was, she said, "more homely." The kitchen is the farm's heart. The house's front door carries you immediately into it. Food is cooked and eaten there and the evening's ceili curls around its ever live fire. It was the Cutlers' kitchen that was decorated with holly and evergreen boughs, providing a setting for the Christmas dinner and play and chat —providing a stage for the mummers.

"*Then there would be the mummers.*

"They used to come around the New Year. You'd be waiting and then you'd hear them coming down the street there."

"Would they be making music, or just noise?" I am sitting close by her. She looks at me and blinks coquettishly to show that my interruption, though a bit stupid, was all right. She answers me and returns to her narrative.

"Just making a noise afore they'd come in, and then they'd knock at the door and they'd say, 'Any admittance for Captain Mummer and his men?'

"I'd go down and open the door to them, and they'd come in and some of them were dressed in women's clothes and big straw hats touchin the ceilin—made out of straw—and some of them might have straw belts on them. And big ould boots and wide trousers and then the Doctor would come in and he'd have a big hat on him and the first man comes in. He'd say:

'Here comes I, Big Beelzebub.
And over my shoulder I carry me club.
Money I want, money I crave,
If you don't give me money
I'll sweep you till your grave.'

Here comes I

"Then this man gets sick. One of them. And the Doctor's called. And the Doctor can cure all aches and pains and the gravel and—och, I couldn't tell you the half of what he could cure.

"And he was lyin on the ground. And the Doctor says to him, 'Get up dead man and fight again.'

"So then, the man would get up. And they'd go through a whole pile of old ramases; I can't mind all what they used to say."

She laughs gently, happily and continues:

"So, anyway, then they had to go around for the money. Coorse, we all give a little to it.

"And they'd thank us very much. And wish us a happy New Year, and away they'd go.

"But before they would go, if they could see a cake of bread on the table or any eatables, you wouldn't have them long; they'd have them with them. I'd say, 'The best of luck to yez.' And away they'd go."

She chuckles, waving an exaggerated adieu to the imaginary mummer who had just fled out the open door and into the summer night, a cake of fadge tucked under his shirt. The tape-recorder hums on the floor at her feet, and I break with her into laughter as she sums it all up:

"So there's the mummers now, and all in a lump and a stack."

On a still, chilling December's night, the mummers would have left the main road and entered the narrow lane that Billy Cutler used to get his donkey-cart of milk to the creamery. Muddy, forest dark, the lane curved before them up the hill. Behind the hedges of trees and thorn, back in the blackness, fell the fields where hay had grown and cows had grazed. Before winter, though, the hay would have been built into pecks in the haggard or piled under sheds, and the milk cows would have been tied into steamy byres. Beating their biceps for warmth, breathing hotly inside the straw helmets that rose from their shoulders, the mummers climbed the lane. The long slow grade grew steeper after they had passed through a gate—the chain holding it was icy to the touch—but their trip was near done. The lane veered sharply to avoid a fairy forth, untouched, tangled in darkness, and forked at the top of the hill, at the corner of the house. One of the lane's branches bent over the Corn Hill toward the farm that lay below, near the bog, the other became the Cutlers' street, its cobbles rough under feet that were numbly wet. On even a cloudless night, the whitewashed stone and crisp thatch of the house would have stood out, coldly, ghostly clear. The mummers passed the byre to the house's door without light, for in winter the window is close-curtained and the door, left open in summer, is shut against the winds rushing down the street and off the hillside. A word of preparation. A knock. And the doorway bursts with the kitchen's brightness. Chairs are shoved back to the walls, and between the hearth and the dresser, their drama begins.

About thirty years have gone. Billy Cutler and Johnny, his cousin who helped in the farm work, have passed on. The two boys who played by the hearth are married men. There are ducks rather than cows in the byre, chickens rather than horses or asses in the stable that extends from the dwelling's other end. Geese for Christmas still fatten in a wooden house down the hill.

Mrs. Cutler places a new stick across the fire. The tongs reflect its pink rising. She sits back and smiles. She has a beautiful smile. "It must have been a great performance," I say. "They'd come up here, come in and say their rhymes." The memory is good to her:

"Aye, indeed. Surely.

"Everyone of them would have a rhyme to say, you see. And the big tall hats touchin the ceilin.

"Ah, dear.

"And one of them used to play a flute or a tin whistle. And they had another one to dance a reel. Do something for their money, do you see.

"They were great, right enough.

"Ah now.

"But they daren't go out now you know. No indeed. Because the last couple of years they were out, they had to get a permit, for since this Trouble they wouldn't be allowed out atall. Masked men in the dark. Not this years.

"No indeed."

The smile with which she began has become a frown. There is daily bad news on the wireless. Belfast lies far to the east but the Troubles are not confined there. The bombs that blow in the town or down along the border echo to her hilltop. People at work on their farms in the soft green Fermanagh countryside have been suddenly, brutally murdered. You never know when the next stranger on the street will be a bitter bastard with a gun. The nights are lonely. The wind howls cold on the street. There is not much money and the work is hard and constant for a woman in her seventies. But she is strong. Last year she whitewashed the entire house, stable, byre, dwelling, all. And she is good-hearted. It is grand remembering when times were calmer and people interacted informally, fearlessly. The young men who went out mumming were mostly from "the other side," as she would say, but they made the long trip up to perform for the Cutlers and they were welcomed when they arrived.

The frown was a momentary lapse, she smiles again:

"Ah, they used to be great, right enough.

"Ah, they were right lads, now.

"I hear tell of them acting the candyman in other houses but they wouldn't do it here now. They were *very nice!*

"Coorse, they were only neighbor lads about, do you know. They knew us. They didn't do anything out of place.

"They came to the door: 'Any admittance?' And then if you'd say no, that there was no admittance, you see, they'd walk away.

"They might say to you when they'd be goin away . . ."

She glances impishly at me, raises her voice and rams the words together as closely as her tongue can get them:

". . . 'Good luck to your cows that your hens may lay golden eggs that your sow might have a hundred pigs.'

"Every one of them would say something to you: 'The best of luck to you.'"

Mrs. Cutler relaxes back in her chair. The smile is still with her:

"Ah now.

"I liked to see them come.

"And Billy liked to see them coming.

"Coorse, there was no lino on the floor that time, and we didn't care what way they came in. Because I used to scrub it out. Twas cement.

"But I loved to see the mummers come. So I did."

The fire shifts into itself. The bottom of the black pot hanging over it glows crimson. Away from the hearth the kitchen is lost in shadow and silence. Outside the door, over the hills and the Lough, the sky is close, dark, soundless. She rises and strikes a match to the gas lamp. The room explodes back into color.

Hugh Nolan:

I'll Tell You the Way It Was

A MATCH FLASH FLUSHES ACROSS MR. NOLAN'S FACE. He draws the flame into his pipe, puffs, and sits back against the fireplace jamb. "Well, Henry, it is time for us to take a sup of tea."

A kettle dangles from the crane crook over the fire. The teapot sits on the table at the back of the kitchen. The bread and butter are safe in a tin by the table under the front window. Our cups, side by side, stand on the dresser opposite the hearth. Making tea would mean much walking for Mr. Nolan. His back is stiff, the clay of the floor uneven. I link the kettle down its chain to get it boiling and spoon tea into the teapot.

As a young man Mr. Nolan pleasured in the company of his elders. He listened closely and rehearsed what he heard over in his mind. He watched the life around him and, being uneasy with writing, filed his observations carefully in his memory. People appeal to him to act as judge in disputes over past events. He is asked to settle bets on the prices of farm commodities and the customs of an earlier time. When questions of land tenure and legacy arise, people come to Hugh Nolan. He is, his neighbors say rightly, a great historian.

The kettle begins to sing. I pour the burbling water over the tea, mash some coals next to the fire into a bed, and set the teapot onto it. The bread is cut, buttered thickly, and piled on a plate. His neighbors told me that Mr. Nolan is a very religious man; they likened him to a monk of old. He sits serenely in his long dark overcoat, bound round with a purple sash. Exactly. Like a scholarly monk from Ireland's gone golden age. Steam waves from the teapot's stroop. I pour the tea over the mound of sugar and synthetic cream in our cups, stir it, and serve the bread and tea to Mr. Nolan. He removes his cap, sets it on his knee, and twinkles me a compliment on my clumsy domesticity.

During the profoundly pleasant days we have spent together he has detailed the work that all men did in his youth. With the first warmth of spring, it was off to the moss ground: nicking and coping, planting and tending potatoes and cabbage and oats so that there would be food on the table and thatch on the roof. The gardens had been hardly begun before the bogs would glitter with the white shirts of men cutting, wheeling, spreading, clamping—winning the turf that kept the hearth red the year through. In all but the best years, the men were up to the meadows before the turf had been brought home to cut, to tedd, to ring and rook the hay that would sustain the cows over the winter. In the heat of the summer most men labored at brick making. Veins of soapy, blue clay ran along the Arney River. It was dug and soughed, slapped into molds, edged, hacked, stacked, crowded into kilns for burning, and loaded onto cots to be shipped down the Lough to build Enniskillen. These slap bricks brought them a little money. Butter and milk brought a little more. There was always the task of following the cows that grazed the upland, and milking those that came to the byre. As winter closed the year down, there was still threshing to be done and perhaps a young beast to drive to the market to finance the pleasures of the Christmas season. Mr. Nolan told it all with a clarity and precision that would cow the proudest prose stylist.

The tea is done. While I rinse the cups, the spoon and the plate, Mr. Nolan glances at the clock on the dresser, moves to the front table, and in the window's light he adjusts the wireless. In silence we listen to the news from Dublin and Derry, Belfast and Washington. Bad news as usual.

This morning we had talked of the battles that had crashed in the locality. Toward the end of the sixteenth century, an

Hugh Nolan: *I'll Tell You the Way It Was*

English army marching from Dublin had been drubbed at the Ford of the Biscuits in the Arney. The carnage was such that some fields about two miles to the west of us are called still "The Red Meadows." A mile to the south at Mackan Hill in 1829 a group of Catholics armed with pitchforks had fought with Protestants who were marching to commemorate William of Orange's victory at the Boyne. Two died. Mr. Nolan arranged the particulars in impeccable sequence, treating the events with the objectivity of the ideal scholar. I was always deeply impressed by his enormous memory and pristine logic.

The news ended, the wireless is snapped off. When battery powered radios first came into use a few years ago, people listened to them constantly, enjoying the "free music" they provided. Soon it was learned that good music—the "real old Irish music"—came over the airwaves but rarely and now radios are left quietly on the kitchen's front table unless it is newstime. To help conversation along, people in Ballymenone maintain a high level of sophistication about national and international politics.

Mr. Nolan returns to his seat and brings the fire to a blaze with a sup of oil. He settles back. The kitchen is dim. Its ceiling and walls surround us in richly textured darkness. One of Mr. Nolan's cats comes to rest purring on my knee. The other sways, almost asleep, in the warmth at the edge of the couch before the hearth. We watch the fire feather and dance. I click on the recorder that sits between us and begin a new topic: "There's another thing I was wondering about, Hugh, and that's mumming. Did you ever go out with the mummers?"

He looks up from the fire. He is an old man deep in his seventies, but his eyes shine, bright as a child's. He provides his own image: his eyes gleam as a sign of his inner clarity.

"No. I never was out with them, but I often seen them, and I often heared their rhymes."

He looks back to the fire in thought. I ask if this kitchen

were a stage for the mummers: "Did they come here to this house?" He answers:

"They did. Oh aye surely. Visited all the houses in the locality."

"Do you remember any of the rhymes?" Though he was not a mummer, his memory is so clean that it is possible he will remember some of their lines. Whatever question I pose, he will pause, then say, "Well, I'll tell you how that was," and launch into a full discourse. He looks down to his right, down into the fire, and draws on his pipe. The clock ticks.

"Well, there was different rhymes, do you know. Every lot of mummers had nearly a different rhyme."

He pauses, puffs. A tractor rackets by, drawing a load of hay bales. The white shirt of its driver reflects a reverse path across the ceiling. The kitchen is dark again. I have learned to wait while Mr. Nolan is doing research. He shifts his pipe from his lips to the fists folded in his lap.

"There came mummers here one time. The first man would come, and he'd tip the door, and he'd say . . . . "

With the beginning of the rhymes, Mr. Nolan modulates into a regular cadence, swinging the words along in near song:

'Here comes I, Captain Mummer with all me men.
Act of young and act of age,
The like of it has never been acted on a stage.'

"So then you'd tell him, 'Come in.' He'd come in. So then the next man he'd call, it be Oliver Cromwell.
"He'd come in and he'd say:

Hugh Nolan: *I'll Tell You the Way It Was*

'*I fought in France,*
And *I fought in Spain,*
And *I'm back to Ireland to fight again.*
And *if you don't believe in what I say,*
Come in Saint Patrick and he'll clear the way.'

"There'll come another man in, and he'll say:

'*Here comes I Saint Patrick.*'

"And I just don't mind the commencement of his rhyme, but Oliver, he says something, and Saint Patrick calls him a *liar*. So he draws his bayonet and he gives Saint Patrick a stab of it, and he falls on the floor."

I had followed the mummers up to the door of Mr. Nolan's whitewashed house by the road. His grandfather built it of local brick. It would still have been thatched then. One by one the characters had ducked through the door and flickered in

He gives Saint Patrick a stab of it

· 15 ·

the light of the kitchen's lone candle. The battle had raged. It seemed reasonable for Ireland's saint to have been trading sword thrusts with Cromwell who occupies a uniquely iniquitous niche in Irish traditional consciousness. And it was reasonable that calling him a liar would engender a fight, for there is no worse insult in this very oral culture. But. Knowing Mr. Nolan's politics are as Green as Mrs. Cutler's are Orange, I ask in surprise, "Saint Patrick dies?"

"Aye. He falls on the floor. So then. The Captain then calls the Doctor. So then. In comes a fellow then and he'd have a black hat on him and a pair of glasses. And he'd have a wee bag with him.
"And the Captain'd say to him: *'What can you cure?'*
"He says he can cure:

'The pain within and the pain without,
The croup and the palsey and the gout.'

"So then the Captain says, 'What are you going to do for this man?'
"Well:

'The livers and lights of a creepie stool.
The spare ribs of a besom.
Give'im that seven times before day,
And if that doesn't cure'im.
I'll look for no pay.'

"Well then. The next man comes in was Little Devil Doubt. So he comes in and he says:

'I'm Little Devil Doubt.
If I don't get money,
I'll sweep you all out.
And if you don't believe in what I say,

Call in Miss Funny,
And she'll clear the way.'

"So then, Miss Funny's dressed up—she's dressed up like a girl, and she comes in and she has a wee bag for the money. So she goes round:

'Here comes I Miss Funny.
Money I want, and money I crave,
And if I don't get money,
I'll sweep yez all away to the grave.'

"So then. She goes round the house. She gets the money. So then. The Captain then calls for a dance. There was a musician with them and he started on a flute or a mouth organ or a piano accordion, if he had one with him, and two of them started and danced a reel.

"So then, they bid goodnight, wished the occupants of the house a happy Christmas and went on to the next house."

Mr. Nolan chuckles gently, while once again I compliment his memory. He smiles:

"Ah, well now. That's not perfect, but it's just as well as I can gather it up. For them that never heard it, it would do rightly.

"There wasn't mummers round this locality for upwards of thirty years.

"You see . . ."

He puts the pipe into his mouth and sucks the flame far into the tobacco. Words return with smoke wisps:

". . . I'll tell you the way it was in the days of the mummers. There was hardly many fellows in the locality had bicycles, and there was none had cars, except a terrible well-to-do man in a good job, you see; well then, the fellows was knockin about the whole winter round, and there was no attractions like what's now, do you see, and they picked up this for a pastime.

"Well, that's a thing of the past now because there's no young lads but they're nearly all in jobs. They're not on the farm, do you see, and then once they're a while in a job, they get a car.

"Well then, when they come home from their work and gets their refreshment, they'll go away again on the car. So there's no combination of young people like what was in days gone by, do you see."

The work Mr. Nolan and others of his generation like Hugh Patrick Owens and Paddy McBrien have described to me was hard, but the work in the bog and at the hay, the terrible labor of the brick making, had all been done by men working in groups. The nights were passed in neighborly chat at ceilis. Times have gotten easier but not altogether better. Quick transport and abundant tobacco do not fully compensate for loneliness. Mr. Nolan has efficiently formulated the theory of alienation. Touched, I agree: "That's right. They don't have much sense of community."

"No. No. And in days gone by, in the winter season of the year, there was no townland but there was a ceiliing house in. And every lad, from he'd quit school (if he got leave from his father and mother to go to such a house) he'd go to it. There bes good sport in it.

"This used to be a ceiliing house in days gone by.

"Well, that has all quit, do you see."

The men who go into the bogs now often do the work of three men alone, but the hay is won by people working in groups. And on cold evenings, the latch of Mr. Nolan's door still lifts regularly as men gather tightly around the fire, warming their palms, smoking and talking until late into the night. The spirit of community has not passed entirely. But groups of young men no longer walk to every house to act out the Christmas drama.

Peter and Joseph Flanagan:

A Little Entertainment

BACK FROM HER STROLL with the other hens, she stands in the doorway. Cautiously stretching one foot, then her beak, then another thin foot, she crosses the wet threshold and perks an eye at us. The sky behind her is the color of old tin. No one moves toward her sack of feed and scraps. It is not yet time for her dinner: she scurries out and around the corner.

The gray light of the front window is mellow over our dinner. "A good feed," P says. "Aye," Joe concurs. And so it is. The potatoes were boiled until they split their skins laughing in the great pot over the fire. They are this year's—new potatoes, fresh from P's garden. It is not possible to stop at one or two. Maybe it's the situation more than the spuds themselves, but their taste seems rich and complete. P passes me the plate, then forks another, deftly skins it, and taps salt over it. My times with the Flanagan brothers in their house at the top of the brae are always pleasing. Peter Flanagan is an artist.

Whenever he arrives where men gather, they will ask for a tune: "Give us 'The Copper Plate' or one of Coleman's reels." His flute is wrapped with brown paper in his inside breast pocket, but P does not always oblige, for he takes his music seriously and wishes to play only for those who can appreciate his talent. He is excellent and has been for longer than a generation. He is beyond the need for new compliments. But should the moment or company be right, he will draw the bright whistle and allow his fingers to fall naturally to it. Quavering and gliding, wild, the notes will rip in ascent. No room could contain the sound: it clatters like a trapped bird at the ceiling and windows, and breaks into sunlight, soaring. Around him the critics will stand, silently in black suits with black stout, staring down into nowhere, their ears cocked the better to hear. They have heard many a man play the tin whistle (there seems to be no public house in the south Ulster hills that lacks its fluter or two) but they will look up, nodding in consensus: there's none better than yer man Flanagan.

Our dinner is done. Joe takes the hens' food to them. P and I settle with cigarettes next to the fire. He brings his body to rest on a low wooden stool. Had he matured in a different world, he could have been a concert flutist or a composer of symphonies. There is music enough in his ear and hand and soul. He grew up, though, on the green hills that roll out of the bogs, and his hands are as familiar with the spade as with the flute or fiddle bow. P Flanagan is a laborer.

Into the workaday chat of the early summer, cold rain had dropped predictions of a bad crop—and worse: the consistent unseasonal chill had reminded everyone of ancient Irish prophecies of the world's end. When the later summer filled day upon day with bright heat, the change was a wonder. Moods lightened as faces reddened and the meadows bloomed with rooks of hay. For over a week, P has been helping his neighbors with their hay, for he owns neither cow nor field. The work is now nearly done and this mizzly day provides him with a chance at a satisfying rest.

It is a relief that the hay has been won, but P lets the agricultural topic fade as he turns to his task of educating me about Irish history. In the past this was one of the Great Days. Doon Sunday they called it and everyone would tramp up to one of the few wild spots left on this controlled landscape—Doon Mountain, beyond Derrylin, where the young people would pick bilberries, sing, dance and court. Our talk skips through the calendar and lights on the Christmas season. Mumming had not entered our earlier conversations, but I know from Mrs.

Cutler that P had been a mummer. He had been, surely, and he would be glad to record the rhymes, just as we had recorded tunes and songs on other days.

Occasionally folklorists recommend sneaky recording, but I have learned that it is best from any perspective to put the machine out in plain view so that the person we strangely term the informant can come to understand and conquer it. I set the machine next to the iron square on which the turf burns, snap it on, check to be certain the batteries are at full strength, and begin by asking when the mummers would go out. He answers:

"It could be around Christmas and it could extend of course as far as the New Year. I think that New Year's Night would be the definite night, the correct night, or even in New Year's Day."

Joe returns to the kitchen and takes the stuffed seat at the opposite corner of the hearth. "Some of them start a week afore Christmas," he adds. P agrees:

"It could start before Christmas, it often did. But the Second Night of Christmas was always the startin time here. It twould be the Second Day of Christmas—Boxing Day.

"And then there was other parts of Ireland, I think, that only done the one day. It was rather a daylight mumming in other parts of Ireland, I understand, and that was on New Year's Day. On New Year's Day. And they would go out and travel that area. Of course, it could be more thickily populated, you see, and maybe more wee towns and villages nearer than what we had. We had only the town of Enniskillen; well, that was pretty far away from us here: it twould be six or eight miles.

"And I think it was really the same in Scotland as well. And they get out and do the one day and wind it up. That finished the procedure.

"We'd keep at it much longer in order to get as much

money—a satisfactory amount to buyin a sufficient supply of drink, you see. And food.

"We went out for a week, went out for a full week, or I might add to that, maybe ten days. Ten nights.

"It wasn't just out to get money personally for themselves; it twas more or less to have a wee bit of a dance, you see, and a bit of a hoolie. Aye.

"They'd have one big dance in a country house, a big party, and have a little of the creatur, as they called it . . ."

Sitting up at the edge of his chair, a hand on each knee, Joe nods his cap and smiles broadly. P laughs aloud, and while laughing keeps on:

". . . accordin to the money.

"A big night that. That was that. That's what the funds went towards now. The whole collection."

The laughter had brought P back on his stool. He flicks the ash of his cigarette into the fire and leans forward, his elbows on his knees, still smiling. I ask him to think back and describe how the mummers would gather.

"Everyone knew of the ould custom, you see, and me and you we'd meet and we'd say, we'll go out the year again. We went out last year and everyone was aware of the bit of sport and the ould customary thing, and we'd all assemble, maybe in a house, an unoccupied house. We wouldn't like to give the occupants of the house any trouble, and we'd say, we'll go to this unoccupied house, and we'd assemble the hats and buy this cotton attire in town; maybe the girls of that district might make the dress for us—the uniform.

"The uniform would be of variegated colors. It twould be cotton. It might be blue. It might be red. It could be any color, and then, of course, there'd be different types of ribbons on it. Oh, very attractive altogether—in such a way that it would entice the people of that district or wherever we'd travel, do you see, that they'd let us in as soon as they'd see us on the street in particular, and we'd be admitted. It twould leave us in that position . . ."

P tilts his head coyly, glancing from the tail of his eye and chuckles:

". . . we'd be more attractive and enticin."

He sits back and returns to the informational mode:

"And then, of course, as well, they knew that this procedure was takin place, you see, and it being a customary thing they'd be delighted to see us and would admit us right away.

"Maybe if you were a person that liked the mummers. Well. You were waitin there and you had the money just on the table ready to hand them. And there were drinks given. And there was tea. We got tea often in houses. They were watchin and there would be a table set. Ah yes, there would be.

"There was some of them really overdone it altogether. They did surely.

"And if you were tired, you could sit down there.

"Supposin you were out the whole long night, you know, from early in the evenin, and come to this house, or go to your house. Maybe you were delighted with the boys' entertainin, you'd let them sit there for as long as they liked. Stay till mornin.

"I seen people puttin us across the Lough there where we done Inishmore. In two boats. Yes. Ferried us across and left us safe. Well, it saved us, you see, maybe the march of two or four miles. That was a big thing after a long day's travelin, you see. A mile means alot when you're tired out.

"Aye."

P pauses, wrinkles his nose and continues. A grave sneer darkens his voice. The words come slowly, violently:

"*And then.* You got the other snig that there was no kick, nor no sport, nor anything in, you see, and they wouldn't like them atall, and they wouldn't admit them."

He sits up abruptly.

"*Well!* There was rules in the mummin squad that you daren't touch anyone. The Captain was responsible for anything that be done.

"If there was any thing done to any occupant—or in the premises around any man's house—well, the Captain would see to that: that that injury would be repaired, and as well that that man—if he was found out during that night or that day that he had done anything, transgressed in any one way— he may get a hidin. And he may get a hidin that he'd lie in bed for a week after. Oh, he would surely. Oh aye.

"So everyone was watched very tightly that they wouldn't commit themselves in any one way. Oh aye surely: because it would give them a bad name, you see, for future Christmases. Oh aye surely: it was really the way: they'd watch that very, very carefully. If they lifted anything in a house, or done anything around a house—outside or in—well: they'd be pulled up for it. Yes. That was just the way. Aye, there were very strict rules in connection with the whole transaction, you see."

Dressed in their cotton tunics with the tall straw cones covering their faces, the mummers were in disguise. "Did the people know who all the mummers were?" P's answer is quick:

"Aw they did. You knew the mummers surely. Why not? And even you didn't know them, you knew they were from the same area not too far away—surely between this and Kinawley.

"And the mummers would know you, do you see, lookin through this straw hat, they'd know you as well as anything. They'd know who was good to them and who wasn't and so on. Oh aye surely.

"And then if they seen that you were friendly, if any of them was hungry or dry, they'd stand at the door and say, 'Give me a drink,' or 'Help us on.' Well, if you had a bottle of stout in the house, certainly you'd take it out.

"Christmas time, you know, it bes a very plentiful time for drink, and maybe you'd give them a bottle apiece, or maybe some of them drinking a mineral. That's the way.

"And then if you saw that they were finishing up here, you know, then you'd say, 'Well, boys, your day's near ended.' And they'd say it was, that this was our last house. And maybe you'd have a kettle there on the fire and the woman wouldn't be ten minutes preparin a sup of tea for them you know.

"That's the way it would wind up."

P is content. The memories remain in a gentle smile. He tosses the butt of his cigarette into the fire, folds his hands. Our friendship and his good humor are strong enough to endure my questions which are mildly abrasive in terms of the local etiquette. The direct question is shunned in normal chat, but I am an ignorant Yank (the notion would horrify my Confederate ancestors) and P deals with my brashness courteously, patiently. I ask how many men would make up the mumming team.

"Well, it would vary in number according to the district of the country. It might be composed of six or eight and it might go as far as twenty. There might be twenty in the bunch.

"Yes, that's the way. So that's it, and we'd all start off and have a musician, either a fiddler or fluter, and a person of course to collect the money, and there and then we'd start off on march with the musician playing. All in step. And we'd go from one house to the other, let it be in the country, let it be on the road, or let it be in the town. Wherever it would be.

"We'd just take every house that we faced, whether we'd

be admitted or not. We'd just take every house that we'd face. Of course, there was people on the other hand that wouldn't admit them because it might frighten youngsters, you see, or cause some confusion. That's the way. That's the way it goes now.

"So. You all stood at the door and . . ."

He twists and rapidly knocks five times on the table.

". . . 'who's there?'

" 'Captain Mummer. Any admission?' Yes, aye, or no: that was the way. 'Any admittance for Captain Mummer and his men?'

"And if the person was pleased to admit you, well, they'd open the door. Throw it wide open for you.

"*And Captain Mummer walked in.*"

P moves quickly from his seat and down the kitchen. His heavy boots sound sharp on the floor. He closes the front door behind him, raps on it thrice, and reenters. He strides ten feet into the kitchen and stands to deliver his lines, turning his torso to project to the audience assembled in a semicircle that runs from the front table past the hearth to the back table. Joe and I are fixed upon him. He is a compact, handsome man.

P is not proud of his tale-telling abilities in the way that he is of his music, but he is a master raconteur, capable of comical impersonations and swift shifts in expression. In conversation he uses two voices artistically. One is low, slow, measured; it is appropriate to serious reminiscence and stories of the weird caprice of fairies and ghosts. The other soars in melodic runs, in looping long sentences that descend to short, punctuating statements. When he recites the mummers' rhymes, though, his voice is set a shade above normal. The words come choppily, without glissandi or variations in timbre. The sound and rhythm are clear, end stops firm:

'Here comes I, Captain Mummer and all me men.
Room, room, gallant room, gimme room to rhyme,
Till I show you some diversion round these Christmas
*   times.*
Act of young, and act of age, the like of this was never
*   acted on a stage.*
If you don't believe in what I say, enter in Beelzebub
*   and he will clear the way.'*

'Here comes I Beelzebub.
In under my arm I carry me club.
In my hand a dripping pan.
I think meself a jolly old man.
If you don't believe in what I say,
Enter in Prince George and he will clear the way.'

'Here comes I, Prince George with my armor shining
*   bright.*
I am a famous champion, likewise a worthy knight.
If you don't believe in what I say,
Enter—'

Frowning, P returns to his stool. It has been years since he has thought of the rhymes. "Let me see now," he says, and sits repeating the speeches of Beelzebub and Prince George under his breath. Joe picks the large turf out of the fire with the tongs and sets them at the front of the hearth. He sweeps the thick ashes off the iron to his side with a besom, places new turf against the backstone, and arranges the old coals next to them. The smoke and glow increase as the new turf ignite. Joe, too, went mumming, but he went out less often than P and cannot remember the part he played. He sits back as P starts in again:

"Beelzebub had a club in his hand and an imitation of a pan. He'd have a sup of water and it'd be drippin off it, if there was any near at hand, you know: 'In me hand a drippin pan. Over me shoulder I carry me club.' He'd have a club with a head on it.

"And Prince George, he'd have a bright band around him, the color of aluminium. And a scabbard here, a holster by his side:

'*Here I come Prince George.*
With my armor shining bright.
I am a famous champion,
Likewise a worthy knight.
From merry England I have come
Many battles I have fought.'

"Wait'll I see now. Ah now it's very hard when you don't mind these things."

He is newly shaved, for they went to chapel this morning. His dark suit is trim. His father was a tailor, a noted musician, a learned man with a fascination for geography. Phil Flanagan is well remembered as "the neatest wee man." Before he died, he moved his family into this house. His two daughters are married and live in New York. Two of his sons farm together near Enniskillen. P and Joe remain. Joe, the older, sits squarely watching P who has wrestled the rhymes into order and brings us in at the start of the fight:

"Then Beelzebub says:

'I swear, be George, you lie sir.'

"And Prince George says to him:

'Pull out your purse and pay, sir.'

"He'll say: 'no!'

He'll slap down on the floor

Joe offers: " 'Take out your sword and try sir!' " P agrees, "Aye" and continues:

'Take out your sword and try, sir.'

'I'll drive me dagger into your side,
And make you die away, sir.'

"Prince George says that. That's what rises the row, and Prince George pulls out his dagger and he drives it into his side, and he'll slap down on the floor. The wounded man. Beelzebub.

"This one they had was a big long knife. You'd swear it was a bayonet. And, be jingo, you'd swear it went into him—the way the spring drives the blade back. And he'll fall, do you see, and let a big groan out of him and you'd swear he was dead."

Suddenly, P clutches an imaginary apron up to his chest and raises his voice into a startling feminine whine:

" 'Ah, God bless us, the puir fellow is dead. Oh what brought yez in here atall atall? I want no one dyin in my house . . . .' "

The woman's distracted keening blends hilariously with P's own laughter.

" 'Run for the clergy for him. Run. Run, run.'
"Bletherin ould lassie: 'Ah, na, na, na, run for the priest, run for the priest. The puir fellow's dead.'
"Says I: 'He's a Protestant.' Says I, 'Don't be runnin for the priest, go down,' says I, 'to the minister.' "

The comical scene dissolves in the laughter that catches us

up and bounds high into the vaults of the roof. The turf sparkles. Our joy quiets into chuckles. Smiling, P says:

"The Doctor is called then:

'Doctor Doctor, ten pounds for a doctor.
Doctor, Doctor, ten pounds for a doctor.'

'Yes, here I come.'

"The Doctor, he'll come. He's dressed up with a bowler hat and a white collar, and, that time of year, a heavy tweed coat, you know, same as any doctor.

'*Here I am a doctor sure and good.*
With my broad sword, I'll quench this man's blood.
If you want this champion's life saved,
Forty guineas I must have.'

'You shall have it, Doctor.'

The vocal tone P uses distinguishes clearly between the Doctor and the other character in the dialogue, Captain Mummer, for the Doctor speaks in the mummers' sing-song, while the Captain strikes a normal conversational pitch.

'What medicine do you use, Doctor?'

'*The fillicifee of a bum bee,*
And the thunder nouns of a creepie stool.'

P smiles. Joe chuckles. We all laugh as P works into the Doctor's rann, submerging the rhymers' cadence in a whippy verbal stream before getting back into step at the end:

'*Mix that* together with a hen's feather and a wran's
      blether.

Peter and Joseph Flanagan: *A Little Entertainment*

Give him that ninety-nine fortnights *before day*.
And if that doesn't cure him, I'll ask no pay.
I have a little bottle in the waist band of me trousers,
Called
Hocus Pocus
Shally shampain;
Rise up dead man and fight again.'

"So he puts down his hand and he rubs the victim on the floor. And he jumps up.

"Miss Funny comes along then. I was Miss Funny the time I was out. I was the treasurer. She's liftin the donations:

'Here comes I, Miss Funny with me big long bag to carry
   the money.
All silver, no brass
If you don't give me money, I'll steal your ass.'

"The musician comes and enters in, and he'll stand in the floor, and, let it be fiddle, flute, or whatever the instrument is, he tunes it up, and the two dancers gets out and gives them a very enjoyable dance. It was always Irish dance music was played, you see.

"And if there's any requests, after, of a song, there's always someone to sing a song—nearly a song to please everybody, no matter who they are.

"That's that, then. They walk out peacefully and on to the next house."

A sense of accomplishment embraces the fireside. We relax warmly. P is a performer of live arts, more than a student of the past, but he has excavated through the strata of his memory, and brushed the dust off a full account of the play in which he had acted. Joe and I congratulate the effort. P picks a coal out of the fire with the tongs, lights my cigarette and then his own.

I ask Joe: "How far did you-all travel?" He swings his arm slowly past the dresser, then points south of the hearth:

"Around here and on round Bellanaleck, you know. Round Druminiskill and up that country."

P draws on his cigarette, rocks forward and expands the mummers' territory.

"We done Inishmore and all the townlands away up around Derrylin and away around Kinawley and around Derrylester, and our last course was Enniskillen. We had to get a permit from the District Inspector to do the town area, the urban area, after doing the rural.

"And that was our last night. The last time that I mummed anyway. Of course, that's quite a number of years ago. That would be away back twenty-five years ago. So it would."

Their area was ambitious. It spread out from their home district, from Ballymenone, where the Flanagans and most of the other mummers lived, but it was not circular. The mummers lept six miles north to Enniskillen and covered Inishmore, an island in Lough Erne, a mile to the east, but their travels were mainly "up" to the south: seven miles along the main road toward Derrylin, and five miles in the direction of the inky mountains, Bennaughlin and Cuilcagh, that brood over the border. They were drawn along lines of cultural and religious affinity toward the well of St. Naile at Kinawley, within a couple of miles of the line dividing Ireland into the North and the State. The southwestern limit of their course ran by a sandbagged military outpost and followed a road that was cratered and bloodstained in the Civil War of 1922. In our years, again, it is the scene of roadblocks, bomb blasts, and twilight rifle fire.

"There was mummers throughout Northern Ireland, but it

was kind of prohibited in the years that there was trouble here in Ireland, you see. Nineteen and sixteen. And it was a kind of prohibited or banned to a certain extent. You had to get permission from the police to go about in disguise or wear-in hoods over your head, you see, that was the reason why. Aye.

"The police would stop you surely. They report, whether it was right or not, that the police could shoot you if they wanted. There was law to shoot any masked or disguised man at that time, you see.

"So then of course that killed that little procedure at that time for quite a long time. Well then, times went on and Ireland got more peaceful. The thing was revived up, you see. Revived up again and it did take a great lead there for fifteen or twenty years, I'd really say, and latterly it has kind of cooled off again now, as all the other Irish customs is just dying out gradually.

"This last few years there hasn't been any of them out. It must be due to the standard of livin raisin in Ireland, and they haven't been out."

With his arms folded, P gazes into the fire. Its patterns vary endlessly. He is one of the few who still wins enough turf for the year's fires. Turf, he says, is composed of matted herbs, so the person who cuts it and the person who sits by its smoke, breathes in the herbs' curative benefit. The smell of the turf burning is sweet. The kitchen is quiet. A rosary and a fiddle bow hang together next to the chimney. The fire darkens. "When did the mummers last come to this house?" I ask of the hearth. Joe responds:

"Well, it would be nine or ten years since they were out in this country. They didn't go out around here. There were people from other districts came in.

"They came by car that time, doin no travelin except through the country. They had their car to bring them around.

"When I went out with them, it was a very hard job, mummin."

P shifts on his stool: "Very hard." Joe: "Travelin at night through the country." P draws on his cigarette and watches the blue smoke curl out of his palm: "Aye, it's very tough, do you know." Joe nods quickly to the side: "They wouldn't do it now." P gestures over his shoulder toward the southeast to a lane leading up from the river bottom, a lane he knew I knew to be a muddy slough on a rainy day:

"You'd be coming up that lane and you'd go up to your knees. It was really mud up to your waist. And you'd have to travel on.

"And there wasn't even the wellington. It wasn't in this country at that time. Twas only the strong, rough, hobnailed boots. Well, you'd have to roll your trousers up to your knees."

It was hard trudging over the hills. Black nights, muddy roads. But you were out with your comrades—the McBriens, the Quigleys, Michael Boyle—the play was fun to put on, and you could look forward to the Mummers' Ball, where all would tumble together for a bright night of warm dancing, fast music, sweet cakes and stout. It was great sport. P's hair curls down over his forehead. He smiles up:

"Ah, they were happy days at that time. Everyone went along. We got money in every house. All sides was delighted.
"They'd like to see mummers every six months at that time.
"A little entertainment, you know. Aw, God, aye. Seeing people perform like that, you know, they were delighted.
"*They were delighted.*"

The clocks on the dresser at the kitchen's other end report that the afternoon has nearly passed. Soon P will insert his flute in his coat pocket and we will be away, through the fields to the car, the road, and a little town south of the border where Fermanagh men gather each Sunday for drink, familiar chat, and music. We will be stopped, we know, by soldiers who will search the car and call us mate alot. The history of our route is well known; its chronicle is one of marching armed men, gunfire, and bombs. We will approach the border by the charred ruins of a customs post along a stretch where innocent men have been cut down in cross fire. It is a risk, but it is worth it. You cannot just sit there looking at the wall, P feels, you need to get out and have a bit of sport with your friends: "Life wouldn't be worth it without a little entertainment."

Michael Boyle:

We Used to Mum in Our Country

HARSH BLUE LIGHT reflects off the floor between the precise rows of white beds. The old men in them lie, unmoving. Some are dozing. Others stare awake, hearing the rasp of their sleeping comrades, the squeaky shoes of the nurse who flits quickly from bed to bed, scratching on a clipboard. Michael Boyle sits up in bed, smoking. His eyes are deep, piercing. He finishes a cigarette, offers me one and takes one himself. I light his then mine.

He was a youthful companion of Hugh Nolan's, a close neighbor of the Flanagans. He is known widely for his knowledge of history. Often I had been told that I should call to see him, but I had been in the area for several months before I found my way through the glossy hospital corridors to his bedside. I returned regularly. Our times together were brief, arbitrarily and unmercifully limited by the bells that signaled visiting hours.

It seemed as though he had been waiting for me. He valued the information stored in his memory and he wanted it preserved. As soon as I would arrive, he would instruct me to get the recorder going; he had been mulling over topics for discussion: he had rehearsed them and was set to start. There was no time for informal pleasantries, no time for solicitous or officious nurses, no time for people who wandered by to gossip or compare illnesses. Our work must go on.

Having finished an account of local ballad making, Mr. Boyle settles back on his pillow. He looks at me, impatient for my next question. His eyes flash. An ashtray, brimming with wrecked butts rests next to him. He is thin. A bad cold fell into his chest while he was thinking more of his farm work than his health, and he has been in bed for nine months. He is very thin, but he is intense and tough.

Michael Boyle, they all said, was the star of the mumming. He was the Doctor, the fullest, funniest role. When the mummers trooped through Enniskillen, he was particularly comical, frightening the little children. "I'll eat you," he would snap at them before they fled.

His hands lie folded outside the covers. I begin to ask about mumming, but once the word is in the air, I have no time to frame an opening question. He rises excitedly on one elbow and is off:

"Oh aye, the mummin. Oh aye, the mummin. I was in the mummin.

"Oh I was a mummer. I was a mummer. We used to mum in our country, nine or ten of us.

"We used to make straw hats, you know, straw hats.

"First, you got a rod, a sally rod, and you made a hoop of it, do y'see. And then you got this straw; you took it like a nice wee handful and you platted it round this hoop, do y'see, and you brought it up to the top. When you done so many, you tie it with a string, do y'see, at the top.

"Like that."

He is sitting up. The straw has been gathered out of the air. He binds it above his left fist with a quick twist.

"And it pulled right down over your face, do y'see, but then you could look out between the wee handfuls of straw and see where you were goin. It covered your face.

"You went into a house, do y'see. You'd see them and know them, but they wouldn't know who you were, when your nose was only out, you see, and you just peepin through it. Aye.

"Well, then you got a bit of some kind of old fancy dress, do y'see. You get a yard or two of what they called cotton—firnical cotton, we used to call it—and you made some kind of a wee jacket, do y'see, and they curved open stripes of ribbons and put on the hat. Decorated yourself, do y'see.

"There was nine or ten of us. There was the Captain and there was a character they called Beelzebub. And there was Miss Funny. She carried the bag, do y'see. Miss Funny. And there was Saint Patrick. There was Prince George. And there was Oliver Cromwell. Then there was a man they called Big Head. He was a musician, do y'see.

"Saint Patrick had some kind of a big gown on him, do y'see, kind of made after the style of a bishop's robe, do y'see, and then he had the ordinary big hat on him that we all wore to disguise his face. And Prince George, do y'see, his armor shinin bright: he had some kind of a lad, you know, like a big white gown on him to shine like armor. Aye.

"Well then: Oliver Cromwell. Coorse, you see, he was supposed to have a big nose stickin out through the hat. Copper nose.

"Well then: I was the Doctor. I had a long black coat on me and a castor hat. They were tall hats. I didn't wear a mask, do y'see. I had the hat on, pulled down, and a bit of an old black veil an old woman gave me over me face. I had a wee travelin bag, you know, that a doctor carries. And I had a big black curving stick. Make meself a kind of a gentleman, you know.

"Then every man had a rhyme to say. Every man had a rhyme. The Captain went in first with his rhyme."

Mr. Boyle slows down, enunciating clearly. He rises to hit each of the rhyming words with particular strength:

'*Here comes I Captain Mummer,*
And all me men.
Room, room, gallant boys,

Michael Boyle: *We Used to Mum in Our Country*

Give us room to rhyme.
We'll show you some divarshion
Around these Christmas times.
Act of young, and act of age,
The like of this was never acted on a stage.
And if you don't believe in what I say,
Come in Beelzebub and clear the way.'

'Here comes Beelzebub.
And over me shoulder I carry a club.
And in my hand a frying pan.
And I think meself a jolly old man
And if you don't believe in what I say
Come in Saint Patrick and clear the way."

'Here comes I, Saint Patrick—'

Apologizing quietly, a nurse breaks in to enter Mr. Boyle
in her census. In the distance, a floor buffing machine whirrs.
Though he is more than twice her age, she speaks to him like
a schoolboy, calling him Michael, pronouncing it in the English
manner—My-kill—rather than the way his friends do—Me-
chull. I am, as usual, annoyed, but I bite my anger back, for
they take good care of him and he trusts them. In my own
nation, with its enlightened tradition of profiteering medicine,
country people of modest means hate and fear hospitals and
are allowed to lie ill, waiting for death alone. With further
soft apologies she leaves, and Mr. Boyle returns, without comment, immediately to the rhymes, repeating Beelzebub's speech
in order to get on the right track:

'Here comes Beelzebub
And over me shoulder I carry a club.
And in my hand, a frying pan
And I think myself a jolly old man
And if you don't believe in what I say
Come in Prince George and clear the way.'

'Here comes I, Prince George,
With me armor shining bright.
I am a famous champion, likewise a worthy knight.
From merry England I have come.
Many deeds I have done.
And if you don't believe in what I say,
Enter in Oliver Cromwell and clear the way.'

'Here comes I Oliver Cromwell,
And the reason I came—'

He stops. "Damnit, I'm gone astray." His forehead furrows.
The man with the buffing machine roars nearer. "Let me see
now." He looks up. "I'll start anew." He repeats the rhymes
of the Captain, Beelzebub and Prince George without change,
and sails smoothly into Oliver Cromwell:

'Here comes I, Oliver Cromwell,
And as you may suppose,
I have conquered many nations with my copper nose.
I have caused the Frenchmen to quiver,
The Scotsman to quake,
And I beat the jolly Dutchman
Till I made his heart to ache.
And if you don't believe in all I say,
Come in Saint Patrick and clear the way.'

'Here comes I Saint Patrick.
And the reason I came,
I'm in search of that bully
Prince George is his name.
And if I do find him,
I'll tell you no lie,
I'll hack him to pieces as small as a fly.
And throw'im to the Devil for a Christmas pie.'

Michael Boyle: *We Used to Mum in Our Country*

'I swear, by George, you lie, sir.'

'Pull out your purse and pay, sir.'

'I'll run my rapier through your side,
And make you die away, sir.'

"So then, Saint Patrick falls, and then the Doctor's called in.
So the Captain calls:

'A doctor, a doctor
Any money for a doctor.'

"And the Doctor comes in then:

'Here comes I, a doctor sure and good.
With my broad sword to stanch this man's blood.'

"And the Captain says:

'What pills do you use, Doctor?'

"So the Doctor says:

'The filliciefee of a bumbee,
And the thunder nouns of a creepie stool,
All boiled up in a woodenleatheriron pot.
Let that be given to him fourteen fortnights *before day,*
And if that doesn't cure'im, I'll ask no pay.'

" *'What can you cure, Doctor?'* the Captain says.

'I can cure the pain within, the pain without,
The little pain,
The big pain,

·43·

The crippin and the palsey and the gout. ·
And I have a wee bottle here in the waistband of me
    trousers.
They call it:
Hokey, pokey
Halicumpain
Rise up dead man and fight again.'

"So then the dead man rises up and that's that. So he calls
then:

'And if you don't believe in all I say,
Come in Big Head and clear the way.'

'Here comes I, Big Head and Little Wit.
The more me head's big, me body's small,
But I'll play a tune to please yous all.'

"So then he pulls out a flute or a tin whistle. He starts playin
and some two fellows starts dancin.
    "Miss Funny, then, she was the last to come in:

'Here comes I Miss Funny,
With a long leather bag to carry the money.
All silver and no brass,
If I don't get money, I'll steal the ass.' "

Mr. Boyle laughs brightly, drawing himself up in bed.

"Well there was different mummers' rhymes all right—
more than them—but them was the ones we used when we were
mummin."

"That's great," I say, handing him a cigarette. He cracks a
match and lights us up. "Who else went around with you?"
Above the buffer's scream, he answers:

"I was the Doctor. I was the Doctor. But John McBrien was the Captain. And there was a fellow named Lunny, Johnny Lunny; he was Beelzebub. He was Beelzebub. Paddy McBrien was Saint Patrick. Benny Quigley, a brother of Paddy's, was Prince George. And Paddy Quigley was, as I remember, Oliver Cromwell. I was the Doctor. Aye. Phil Flanagan, a brother of P's, he was Big Head. And P was Miss Funny, he gathered the money.

"The two Quigleys and two Flanagans and me. There was three McBriens. There was Paddy McBrien and John McBrien and Jemmy McBrien. John and Paddy's livin yet. Jemmy's dead. There was meself. I was the Doctor.

"Them was the mummers."

Dredging the rhymes up onto the decks of consciousness had taken great concentration. With subdued jubilation, Mr. Boyle announces, "Aye, them's the rhymes." He remains buoyant. "Would you-all get together and practice before you went out?"

"We did. We'd get together. We'd gather up in some house and make the hats and practice, you see, and decorate ourselves.

"A couple of night's practice would get them all. Two nights. Three or four nights would get them all."

He taps the ash off his cigarette. The mad buffer has retreated. A radio somewhere mumbles on, recounting last night's roster of explosions. "Would one person remember all the rhymes?"

"Yes. It was an old man named Owens. He lived down in Clockareddy. And he had the rhymes and he wrote them out for us.

"He did. He wrote them out for us and we learned them. He was the man put us on the road. He had the rhymes, do you

All silver and no brass

Them was the mummers

see. Oh, he had a great head. Very smart man. And he gave every man his rhyme. We learned them as he wrote.

"Well, Owens, he was an old man like in that time and he had them on down from his ancestors.

"We'd go out, we'll say, of a Monday night. And we'd mum for about five nights before Christmas. About five or six nights.

"We went to every house. Ah, we traveled to every house in the district and away out of it too, do y'see. We used to get money in every house. Not an awful lot, but six pence and a shillin, and then we had a big dance, and we bought sweet bread and tea and sugar, and had a dance. Not an awful lot of drink at it. But some, do y'know. We wanted it anyway.

"Ah, if you got three or four pound that time you could have a powerful spree, do y'see.

"If you got three or four pound you had a powerful do. Aye. We had a powerful do all right. If you had a few pound that time you had a great do.

"Got a house from someone, do y'see. We had a grand spree around the Christmas time. It would sometimes be the Second Night and often later. It was always of a Sunday night or the Second Night of Christmas. Aye, it used to be a great way to get entertainment. The best sport.

"They'd be watchin for the mummers for a week before Christmas, and they'd be delighted to hear tell of them comin, and be all ready for you.

"You'd nearly always get refreshments. Get tea, do y'see. There was none of us at the time hardly takin a drink. We were all young lads. Eighteen or nineteen; that was the age we were. We weren't much interested in drink. But we'd take tea. Oh aye.

"There would be tea in some houses. We wanted it for travelin about. You want refreshments all right. We walked plenty.

"Aw, it was great sport. It was a bit hardship at the same

time. Generally, you'd get bad weather about that time and often a bit of a rough night.

"We didn't mind it; we were all young.

"We didn't mind it. We were all young."

When I first met Mr. Boyle he had contrasted today's world with that of his youth. The people now travel in cars. They pass anonymously on the roads, moving too quickly to appreciate the beauties of the countryside or to find a moment for talk. No time is left from their efforts at money making for a friendly night's ceili. In the days of the mummers, "they were poor," he said, "but they had comfort and sport." Each time I saw him he looked fitter. He said the frequent talks about good times in the old days had done more for him than the doctor's medications. When I stopped to see him just before my return to America, he was sitting up in bed, fully dressed in a suit and a tie. Color had risen in his cheeks. He was planning to be home for Christmas.

RHYME

AND REASON

Survival

Geography

Performance

Meaning

Function

Survival:

The Ould Customary Thing

The Celtic Twilight begins with young W. B. Yeats telling his reader to expect neither theory nor explanation. His intent is to set country people, their beliefs and arts, on the page, "unoffended or defended by any argument." The poet's small book lets Paddy Flynn stand out on his own. But from his autobiographies we know Yeats had his reasons, his arguments.[1]

He went into the countryside to clarify his thinking on radical nationalism. Complete submission to the movement rolling toward the Post Office at Dublin on Easter of 1916 would yoke his purposes with those of a militant, pragmatic, Catholic lower class. Gentle, angry Yeats came of a comfortable, if unorthodox, Irish Protestant home. He went into the countryside to simplify the diction of his early poems. They were, he felt, too florid, too Victorian. The aesthetic of the country people was purer, more primal. He hoped the folk arts would lead him to an artistic wellspring where he could drink to transcend the complicated materialism of the nineteenth century arts. He went into the countryside to mystify his being. The country people knew the tricks of the lock on one of the doors opening into the spiritual world. Yeats tried constantly to enter that other sphere—through hashish and Oriental philosophy, through his wife's automatic writing, through conversations with Madame Blavatsky and a hypnotist who had lived with the Zuni, through folklore collecting among the Sligo peasants.

William Butler Yeats thrilled to the poetry of William Morris in which heroes rode again to explain a world more beautiful than the alienated, industrial age into which Morris and Yeats had been unhappily thrust. Yeats' sister embroidered the hangings on Morris' bed, he dined with Morris, and adopted his socialist politic. Morris' message was unity.[2] He imagined a medieval past when art and labor, spiritual and material concerns were fused. "Unity of Being" became the driving force in Yeats' life, his religion. Like Morris he was horrified by the fragmentation of modern times, but he held hope for the future. Years later, depressed, he gave poetic cloth to his thought that the loss of innocence and sincerity had set the stage for a terrible Second Coming.[3] A line from his poem by that name gave Chinua Achebe the title for his fictive description of the disintegration of Nigerian traditional life, *Things Fall Apart*. In *The Celtic Twilight*, though, Yeats was content to limit his overt argument to its closing two paragraphs in which he reaffirms the philosophy of William Morris.

Yeats knew why he assembled bits of folk wisdom into a book. Country people gave him what Morris had discovered in medieval tapestries, churches, and poems: a reflection of a more unified age, clues to the construction of an alternative to modernity. He did not, however, push that message aggressively through his writings on folk culture.

Undefended, Yeats' country people depended for their acceptance upon the good hearts of their readers. The young James Joyce, whom Yeats compared to Morris, admired Yeats' work in general and *The Celtic Twilight* in particular. But this was because he sensed in it an ironic distancing between Yeats and his subjects. Yeats truly wished to be one with the people, but some delicate ambivalence—sprung from his raising or religion or affection for erudition—prevented him from breaking the last barriers away. Joyce, with his liking for popular arts and distaste for "the Irish rabblement," looked into Yeats' book and found his own image mirrored there. When he came upon similar folk stories offered blandly by Lady Gregory, his reaction was quite different. Yeats, whose work inspired Lady Gregory, called her book "beautiful." Joyce called her stories senile, the expressions of "feeble and sleepy" minds. Lady Gregory, too, published folklore texts with "no theories, no case to prove."[4]

Like the tales Yeats and Lady Gregory collected on their trips together through Galway, mumming was important. With a little effort, men in Ballymenone now remember the text and social ambiance of a play that has not been performed for a quarter of a century. They enjoy thinking and talking about it. Mumming is very important to them, but the reasons are not all apparent. It is not enough to present accurate texts of unfamiliar artworks, for readers will reject or rationalize them on the basis of some facile, tacit principle. As folklorist, my duty to my human constituency and their patrimony is honest presentation—and serious, ethically restrained study. What the folklorist, like myself, owes his readers is not an easy model that lulls them into believing the world is just as they thought it was. I must keep the world strange while helping you discover it. That requires inquiry, analysis, and interpretation.

As he moved into his influential interpretation of mumming, the medievalist E. K. Chambers commented that "it is, after all, the origin of the play, rather than its latter end, which is of interest to the folk-lorist."[5] Much has happened in the generation since Chambers wrote. We folklorists have lost our hyphens and our theoretical innocence; our interests lie more in latter day dynamics than speculations about origins.

In line with other modern thinkers, contemporary folklorists wish to understand acts and arts in their own terms— the terms of their performers, their audiences, traditions and conditions. But most of the mumming scholars are still off questing for holy origins. Their journeys continue to be guided by academic maps drawn up by the lesser thinkers of the period of Morris and Yeats.

In the modest address he gave after receiving the Nobel Prize, W. B. Yeats said the imagination and speech of modern Irish drama were founded upon a medieval poetic that had survived among modern country people. Yeats enjoyed connecting Irish rural beliefs with those of ancient and medieval people and he commented, a little facetiously, that he could track any good modern folk expression back to classical times. He did not, though, formulate this interest into a theory and was amusingly critical of folklorists who, in an effort to be scientific, ignored the voice and pulse of the people during their search for the "primitive religion of mankind."[6]

The anthropologists and folklorists of the nineteenth century could not help but be affected by the romantic philosophies announced with such fury and beauty by thinkers like William Morris. Parts of the romantic message they left aside. Other parts they connected with the prevailing scientific concern of evolution and built into a theory of survival. Foreign societies were viewed as relics from man's social beginnings. Folk arts were viewed as relics of prehistoric spirituality. We call these old thinkers the survivalists and could leave them on their antiquarian perches high in our family tree, were it not for the survival of their ideas within modern works on mumming.[7]

The prime concept of the survivalist theorists of mumming has its source in Sir James Frazer's *The Golden Bough* and parallels the thinking of those scholars who locate the origin of all myth in ritual—an idea that fares miserably today.[8] Once upon a time, we are told, there was a fertility ritual that efficiently structured the agricultural year by means of magical mimicry. Latter day mumming is but an irrational fragment of this ritual, having drifted into modern times through the inertia of the peasant mentality.

For a long time it has been fashionable to dismiss survivalism as a Victorian embarrassment. But the elder scholars were intellectuals and they were not cowards. Two things need saying in their behalf.

The first is that one element in their guess could be right. There may well have been a cyclical fertility ritual of which the modern mumming is a descendant. Nobody knows.

A second matter is this. All things are expressions of ideas held in the minds of their makers, and these ideas are formed out of other, necessarily older ideas. Although it is a static way to describe cognition, all things are, in a way, survivals of earlier things. Cubistic painting might, accordingly, be seen as a survival of realism, for aspects of the cubistic canvas— subjects and images, techniques and design—are continuous with older practice. Modern folklorists often operate in imitation of the anthropologists of a generation ago who studied nonliterate people as if they were gears in some clock without hands. At least the old survivalists did not ignore history, as some modern folklorists try to do.

Men rarely go out mumming today. Folklorists are not historians, so they see little need to study things like mumming. It is dead, they say, and there is little need to study dead things. Actually, there are good reasons. Without the past, the present is incomprehensible. The best one can do is to reduce the present to an elegant metaphor and kick up a grand rhetorical fuss about dynamics. It has been a long time since P Flanagan and Michael Boyle tramped the damp lanes in costume. Folklorists cannot observe their play now, but that does not mean it is dead. Events in the past, held in the memory, can be as influential upon people's actions as events in their immediate contexts. Memory is a behavioral reality. Mumming lives forcefully in the minds of Ballymenone's old mummers and it provides a strong supporting argument in their angry critique of modern existence.

If the survivalists did not ignore history, neither did they understand it. The human beings in their schemes, like those manipulated by some current scientistic scholars, are witless puppets, rather than history's products and producers. And the survivalists did ignore a main concern of modern students of humanity—that of alternative systems of logic. Cubism may be a survival of realism, but that does not mean the cubistic depiction is less reasonable than the realistic one. Or more reasonable. Mumming does have a long history, running back to the seventeenth century and possibly beyond to a misty pre-Christian dawn. There is a description of mumming from the city of Cork, in 1685, and a wealth of suggestive references from medieval documents.[9] In its original setting, whatever it was, mumming made sense. But in its most recent setting it made sense too.

Given their times, it is no surprise that the survivalists spent their energies hunting origins and were unable to make sense of the drama as it existed in their day.

If they went out into the countryside, they would meet sweet, intelligent old men and women who could surrender up to them the poetic treasures of the Middle Ages. They would also encounter rough, hard people, digging wearily in the dirt, agitating for the Land League, advocating the murder of the landlords, brawling at country fairs, roaring from house to house at Christmastime coercing the inhabitants into giving them money to keep their drunk going. It was easiest to snatch a naked text, no questions asked, and return to the cozy study. There, amid familiar volumes, they could stuff their pipes and invent nicer actors for the play. The peasants of the present, they felt, were dull and incapable of understanding their own actions, but the original players were contemplative and logical. They may have been philosophical, those dim, primitive mummers, but they were fearfully sombre.[10] They could not doodle a design on a barn door except as a superstitious symbol. They could not ramble the countryside putting on a play to have a good time, they must have been striving to insure the growth of the crops or the return of the sun. The survivalists made up the original mummers to look very much like themselves.

It was not only the early students of mumming who removed themselves aloofly from real mummers. One recent scholar termed "comic" and "delightfully comic" the fact that mumming was banned by the police on the Irish border.[11] He can have no awareness of the importance of the play to its people, nor any feeling for the conditions the people of the countryside endure.

Survival: *The Ould Customary Thing*

The survivalists of our day or Yeats' are not satisfied with eliminating the performers from their studies. To justify their interest in origins they find it necessary—so necessary that it appears a bit defensive—to attack the play as it flourished when Michael Boyle played the Doctor. "Fragmentary," they call it: "nonsensical," "garbled," "undeveloped," "puerile," "incoherent," "corrupt," "degenerate."

The old-time scholars were comfortable with those adjectives because of their elitist ethic. And because of their realistic aesthetic. Even after the modernist revolution of Joyce and Kandinsky, we remain most comfortable with the full realism of the nineteenth century, with a painting that represents something out there, with a novel that tells a story. It is no wonder, then, that the scholars of the past preferred long narrative folksongs and tales. When they came upon an abstract piece of theater like the mumming it was natural for them to imagine that it might once have been a fuller work, portraying not only a death and rebirth, but—in order to accomplish its magical mission more efficiently—the entire human life cycle laid out in neat sequence like an eighteenth century biographical novel. Viewed from the tower of their taste, mumming did look like a fragment.

It is not altogether wrong to call the mummers' play fragmentary. Each thing is part of some larger thing. The statue of a saint is part of the facade of a cathedral which is part of a city. The same statue is also part of the aesthetic and religious thinking of its sculptor and viewers. Mumming, like the statue, was but a fragment of spatial, temporal, and mental continuities. Still, the thing that is a fragment exists, simultaneously, as an object in itself. The sculpture or even the saint's stone eye can be imagined alone. Mumming was part of the Midwinter season in Fermanagh, and Midwinter was part of the year's cycle of events. But the play was a separable whole with its own phenomenal integrity. Midwinter passes now without mumming and the mummers can break into your mind on a soft summer's evening.

The play was torn from the ordinary. It began with a knock. People calling to ceili in Ballymenone do not knock. The door is open in the summer. In winter, the latch is lifted and the kitchen is entered directly. Even strangers, like myself, are not expected to knock and they are not asked their business until they are inside and next to the hearth. The kitchen is continuous with the house's street; it exists between the public space of the road and the private spaces hidden behind closed doors at each of the kitchen's ends. The play closed with a formal greeting, a wish for a happy Christmas, though the casual ceilier leaves with little ado. It was a special event.

The players were costumed. They spoke in rhyme and rann. Their entrance and exit, their appearance and sound, all removed them from daily life, welcoming a suspension of the usual, and calling attention to the play as an independent entity.

The drama's sparse poetic emphasizes its independence. Like the ancient ballad, mumming is constructed of repetitious, manneristic speeches and tersely motivated violence. Circumstantial detail, intricate character development, and flurries of words are nice to find in a book read once, but a lean and surreal quickness is an effective dramatic solution for a play that is performed perhaps thirty times a night for ten days at a stretch, that is seen annually throughout a lifetime.

The elder ballad scholars were apt to call their longest texts "good" and their short ones "fragments." Some short texts are, indeed, scraps wrenched from the imperfect memories of friendly old people. But others come from sensitive singers who have boiled a prolix narrative down to its emotional essence.[12] I well remember Ola Belle Reed, a superb traditional singer from the North Carolina Blue Ridge, receiving a hand-written copy of a ballad and instantly striking out half its stanzas as being unnecessary to the song's story or its impact.

Although it is often said that the modern mumming is the detritus of a long realistic drama, it would be better seen as an intensification, a perfection—a streamlining. If the play once told the whole story of a human life, the Ballymenone mumming is not the survival of a random segment, but a concentration upon life's central mystery: death. A more reasonable candidate for the longer original from which the modern play could have come would be a play with a series of combat scenes. Plays of the sort have been found in Britain and in the West Indies where they enjoy especially joyous elaboration.[13] These longer plays only multiply the idea quintessentially available in the Ballymenone drama.

Emotional intensity, rapid action and minimal characterization are crucial to the effect of both ballad and mumming. Different audience members are allowed personal interpretations of the message while sharing in an experience of poecy and form. The mummers' audience cannot easily miss the similarity of characters who dress and speak nearly alike and nothing like us: if the mummers represent something, it is not real people.

As is the case with the ancient tale, repetition shoves the play's basic structure to the surface. No subtle analysis is required to trace its geometry. It is made of an opening procession, balanced by a closing procession ending in a dance. Between the processions, there is a stylized challenge, fight, and ressurrection. The combat is doubly framed to heighten its unreality, decreasing anxiety and increasing wonder in its audience.[14] There is no mimesis, no intention to duplicate life as it flows. The play is artificial, symmetrical, fantastic.

The scholar trained to favor the illusionistic arts, the paintings of Raphael, the novels of Dickens, was not prepared to appreciate the mummers' play. But the scholar of the twentieth century should be.

As our century began, Yeats, who called himself the last romantic, wrote a set of essays on the present and future of poetry and drama. Although he happily contradicted himself, there is a logical structure in those early writings which is also to be found in the works of William Morris and John Ruskin, Morris' early mentor.[15] I will name it the Romantic Argument.

It runs like this: The High Renaissance unleashed the slumbering violence of individualism which, as manifested in the rationalism of the eighteenth century and the materialism of the nineteenth, has separated man from man, art from life, and sundered the arts into hidebound categories. The hope for humankind is to search for unity, harmony. Since the contemporary world has become so fragmented, harmony cannot be found on the surface of things but must be sought in the deep unseen where art and life are guided by the same laws. These timeless first principles of life and art can be located in the self by contemplation of the works bequeathed to us from a more integrated, pre-Renaissance period or by experiencing the life of people whose traditions put them in touch—if only in a disturbed, melancholy way—with that earlier, more perfect time.

It was the survivalistic term in this Argument that the nineteenth century folklorists and anthropologists accepted. Recently, we have come to recognize the importance of its midsection. For years we followed the programs of the seventeenth and eighteenth century philosophers and looked at culture as a list of institutions and traditional art as a list of genres. Accumulation, classification, and enumeration—gathering, splitting, and counting—seemed satisfactory ends. There are many indications of our newfound desire to shake free from an archaic rationalism, but the clearest are to be read in the current enthusiasm for linguistics and the linguistically inspired structural anthropology of Claude Lévi-Strauss.[16] The important truths, says Lévi-Strauss, are not to be found at the ephemeral phenomenal surface of things but in the timeless interdependent principles of transformation lying deeply beneath them.

These new developments in folklore and anthropology, however, are old ones in art. The artists of the first twentieth century generation rejected the part of the Romantic Argument that the early folklorists and anthropologists accepted, and developed modernism out of the parts of the Argument that we social scientists are currently embracing in an attempt to drag our disciplines into our century. We have finally awakened to the view of reality propounded by the great moderns, men like James Joyce.

The bomb Joyce lit in *Ulysses* exploded in *Finnegans Wake*. A book that begins and ends in the middle of the same sentence, that incessantly reorders scraps of any reality according to nonlinear, fundamental principles, the *Wake*—"monomyth" it calls itself—is the realization of the closed, transforming system of infinite power that the contemporary structuralists hold as an ideal.[17]

Like Claude Lévi-Strauss, whose theories of *bricolage* and mediated opposition can be neatly adumbrated in the *Wake*, James Joyce did not love modern painting. Still, the articulate painters of his period were working toward his symphonic synthesis and were comparably anticipating the structuralist program.[18] Wassily Kandinsky and Paul Klee described their new, nonobjective art as more spiritual than material, more harmonic than melodic, more simultaneous than sequential. Emancipated from the order of the phenomenal world, the new art was not, they said, a distorted presentation of natural form: it was the result of participation in natural forces, the exposure of inner relations, the attempt to present for view unobservable but nonetheless real dynamics.

The early moderns, like the great romantics before them, hated their materialistic era and worked subversively to hasten the arrival of a better future, but they did not feel the only escape led backward to Morris' Middle Ages or outward to Yeats' Sligo. Any exit was worth a try. Yeats chided the younger poets who considered jazz and music hall ditties to be folklore and worthy models for a modern art. But James Joyce not only incorporated pop kitsch, he used Yeats himself, and, it seems, about everything else to create his cyclic vision in *Finnegans Wake*. Art, Yeats felt, must be in some measure restrained, but Joyce's *Wake* is so personal that all the learned professors in the MLA will never get it back together again.[19] The modern movement was expressionistic. Its painters and poets broke all the rules, expressing themselves without regard for tradition or audience. It ended in black canvases and silent symphonies.

Sometimes it embarrasses us, but we folklorists are the heirs of the romantics. Our new theories are theirs, refracted through modernism. Like them, we still search for the authentic outside of ourselves in folk art. While the world changed fitfully, we sought the authentic in the perduring, the timeless, the traditional. Now, in a time of efficient mass communication, we are seeking the authentic in artistic, symbolic, face-to-face encounter. This does not block our entrance to modern times, though, for not all the moderns neglected the folk arts. Some saw that what they were trying to accomplish had already been achieved by artists of tradition. "Finnegan's Wake" is the name of a folksong. Frank Lloyd Wright built his modern architecture upon a convenient reading of Ruskin and Morris and wrote early in his career that, "the true basis for any serious study of the art of Architecture still lies in those indigenous structures; more humble buildings everywhere being to architecture what folk–lore is to literature or folk–song is to music . . . ."[20] Kandinsky recognized African carvers of masks and peasant painters on glass to be his brothers in art.

Wassily Kandinsky used folk art to help him invent the future of painting, and his experiences can help others locate the qualities of traditional art.[21] Folk art is like modern art. It is not abstract in order to be decorative or in order to misrepresent the visible world. Its repetitiousness, simplicity and seeming unreality come out of its authors' sincere attempts to express a resonance between a spiritual inner sound and an outward materiality. The usual critic, because he is not an artist, can find excellence in an artwork only when it displays obvious originality, so he has difficulty in apprehending the qualities in folk art. But Kandinsky, the painter, knew that an artist who hews tightly to tradition's line can create fine art, if his art is committed, if his artwork arises naturally from inner need.

To be great, art need not be original or unconventional, it needs only to be authentic.

With Kandinsky's writings we are beginning to find a mood proper to the examination of the mummers' play. Searching for comparable modernist manifestos written expressly for the theater, I came upon the strange, flaming book, *The Theater and Its Double* by the poet, Antonin Artaud.[22] Like the later works of Joyce, Kandinsky, and Lévi-Strauss, Artaud's new theater was conceived in opposition to the materialistic, empirical realism of the nineteenth century. The new theater will not be built of endless dialogues in which psychological mysteries are reduced to facts; it will unfold in music and dance, poetry and humor, in improbable, symbolical violence. It will be a theater of delight, of vague, profound terror.

Artaud gained little support for his thinking from classical Western drama, but he could cite traditional Balinese theater for authority. The playwright Bertolt Brecht was similarly inspired by Chinese theater while developing his aesthetic for modern drama. Brecht's design was to present finished, controlled, subtly unrealistic performances, incorporating song, dance, and mime to induce sensations of strangeness and detachment in the audience.[23] Like Brecht and Artaud, and years before them, Yeats had become fatigued with bourgeois theatrical realism and like them wishing something simpler, more integrated, more archetypal, he had turned to an Oriental model. From the traditional theater of Japan he took the idea that poetry could be performed: it could be sung and danced by masked players moving near their audience in a stylized manner without elaborate sets or props.[24]

Yeats did it. He draped an ancient Irish theme over the form of a Japanese Noh play. Sean O'Casey saw it. He went to Yeats' home in Merrion Square in Dublin and watched a performance that was charming and graceful, he felt, but not vivid or Irish enough.[25] That was just the sort of criticism Yeats would have offered twenty years before.

Noh plays were too removed from the Celtic spirit, even as it faded in twilight. The mummers' play was, perhaps, too close. But it could have provided modern dramatists with guidance like that Kandinsky found in peasant painting, for it was spectacle of the kind they imagined: manneristic, poetic, strange. Captain Mummer tells us his play is not from the tradition of classical Western drama: "The like of this was never acted on a stage." It would be more equitable to judge mumming on the criteria of the modernists than upon those held by Victorian realists. Like the theater of Artaud (or the myths of Lévi-Strauss), mumming emerges as the interval between the concrete and abstract closes. With *Finnegans Wake*, it pitches mythically between dream and awareness. Mumming is not a theoretical, symbolic art like a medieval morality, nor is it an empirical, descriptive art like a play by Ibsen. It rises between these poles of Western thought, falsifying their purity, uniting them in mysterious imagery.

Before Joyce had completed the *Wake*, Samuel Beckett warned us to resist the temptation to kill its art by reducing it to a theoretical system or a mere description of the dream state.[26] I do not want to murder mumming by explaining its soul away and offering its tabulated innards up to science. But I do wish to examine it closely in order to enrich our experience of it. So, I have set up an intellectual backdrop against which we can view it and I plan now to explore the sense it made in Ballymenone. Our discoveries may have broad implications, but in other places similar plays fit into similar cultures differently.

To get at the sense of the play, to develop a defense for it and its players, I had to become offensive. The first long conversation on mumming I had with Ellen Cutler, Hugh Nolan, Peter and Joseph Flanagan, and Michael Boyle, is the one I reported in this book's earlier chapters. I could not, however, stop at one conversation. I had to think about what they had said and return to the topic time and again during our many visits. They, of course, found it easiest to put the verbal parts of the play into words, but I needed to understand its nonverbal parts too. Like social scientists, they tended to generalize on the basis of a few specific memories. They all apparently remembered one presentation of the play most clearly. So, I had to push them over the same matters several times to approach the underlying principles of performance. With repetition, their memories and my understanding filled out. Fortunately they like talking about mumming, so the friendship I cherish far beyond the information was not endangered by my picky interrogations.

Geography:

A Custom in These Islands

Early in our century an English gentleman traveling in northern Greece was given a description of a play traditional to that area. On Epiphany a group of boys come to the door and knock. If they are not admitted they prank about the house, stealing, damaging, and cursing in song the householders' hopes: "Master, in your dirty little house, full of crows, half are laying eggs, half are hatching them, half are pecking out your eyes." If admitted, they enter and arrange themselves in a semicircle. A chorus sings, wishing its audience well, while one boy, dressed as an Arab, makes untoward advances upon another, dressed as a Bride. The Bride's Groom, understandably indignant, engenders a quarrel, whereupon the Arab kills him. The Bride weeps, then calls for the Doctor. Dressed in collar, black coat and hat, like a graduate of Athens University, the Doctor administers to the deceased who hops up and joins in a dance. The play ends in a sexual pantomime by the Bride and Groom, after which the head of the house gives the boys money or food and wine and they leave, feeling free to steal a chicken as they go.[1]

By formulating an abstract description of the Ballymenone mumming we can see that it is similar to its Greek contemporaries. However, the closer we look at the play, the closer we will be to its home territory. Through comparison, the play provides us with an index to the geographical identity of its players.

Traditional dramas with processions, battles, death and resurrection, were performed widely in Europe, but it is not until we come upon the hero-combat plays of Britain that we find a close relative of the Ballymenone drama. Many of the plays acted out in Scotland and England are structurally identical and verbally quite similar to the Ulster ones, but when Saint Patrick and Oliver Cromwell appear in the play we can be pretty certain we have an Irish text. If the drama is further elaborated to include Irish patriots like Brave Dan O'Connell, it comes from Wexford in Ireland's southeast. When the combat in an Irish play involves Saint George and the Turkey Champion and the offerings are gathered by Johnny Funny, the play lies close to northern English tradition and most likely comes from eastern Ulster. In the east, Patrick is also frequently a combatant, but if Oliver Cromwell is a swordsman, as he is in Hugh Nolan's description of the play, and Miss Funny takes up the collection, we have almost surely arrived in southwestern Ulster, in the hills near the Fermanagh-Donegal border.[2]

The geographical perspective we gain through abstraction and comparison is not unavailable to the participants of the mumming. Like many Irish men, Hugh Nolan had worked awhile in Scotland; he comments:

"Mumming has been a custom in these islands. In Scotland, they used to always have the Hogmanay men. They used to go out before New Year's Day and go through the same performance as they did in this country.

"In Scotland they did the whole celebration on the one day: on New Year's Day."

Peter Flanagan and his fellow mummers learned that they shared their tradition with Scots in a different manner. If they traveled to each house in the area, eventually they would come to the mansion of the Church of Ireland rector, set east of Bellanaleck. The ensuing performance, like that which was interrupted by the woman who thought a real blow had struck a man dead to her kitchen floor, became integral to P's recollection of mumming. On each of the three occasions that we spent several hours together on the subject, he offered a version of the anecdote about the wailing woman and this one about the rector:

"The mummers went under different names. They were called the straw men or wren men. They were called mummers. They were called Hogmanay men. They went in under different names.

"They never got the Hogmanay men name here. It was Scotland.

"I remember goin—we were doin Bellanaleck district, you know—we went into the rector who was the name of the Reverend Lapham.

"And the Captain asked, of course, for admittance: 'Good night, your Reverend sir, we are mummin, would you like to admit us?'

" 'Oh,' he says, 'Yes, I will, surely. I'd love,' he says, 'to see yous. I often heard,' he says, 'tell of the Hogmanay men.' That was the first I heard of it.

"And, of course, he had a lovely place. Rugs up to your knees. And we were nearly ashamed to be admitted atall, or to go in, you know. Strong boots on us. Probably mud on them.

"Oh, it didn't make one bit odds what nuisance we caused or anything else as long as we went through our performance. He was delighted. So we did it to perfection. And *he was delighted*. He said he never saw anything in his life he liked as well or cherished as much as what we did. Aye.

"He put his hand in his pocket and he gave us ten shillings. It was a big thing at that time because it was only a shilling you would get: if you got a shilling you were pleased: two shillings was the general run. He give us ten.

"Well, we praised that clergyman to all admiration. He was a terrible man. We prayed for him to get Heaven. If he hasn't got Heaven, it's not our fault.

"Reverend Lapham can't blame us.

"A nice old man."

Laughing a little still, P pauses and Joe adds: "Likely he has gone through the gates afore this." P smiles:

"He was a nice, a gentle man. He was. Very, very nice man: the Reverend Lapham."

P Flanagan believes mummers performed throughout Northern Ireland, and most areas in Ulster did have their mumming teams. He knows mummers went out all around his locality. This meant that the area mummed had to be marked out and oral treaties had to be made with men from other places. A proviso of these treaties would be that each team would invite the other to its Mummers' Ball. P tells us:

"We would do a certain area, and we'd know where the other ones was and how far they'd come. We wouldn't just infringe on their district, you see.

"Supposin now there was another mummin crowd up Derrylin and they were comin on down this way past here, we'll say to, well roughly round Kinawley.

"Probably we'd hear that, and they might send word that they were comin down. Well, we wouldn't step in on their area and we'd do on the northwest side there on around. And we'd do this other part on around by Inishmore. There might be another crowd out beyond the Lough doin in another area.

"There was circles, you see. There was mummers throughout all Northern Ireland."

Recognizing that mumming was not unique to them, provided the men with a sense of connection to a broad cultural region, spreading beyond Ireland to Scotland. At the same time, their local identity was reinforced by the knowledge that their particular rhymes were different from those of any other men. Hugh Nolan had begun his exposition of mumming by noting that each group had "nearly a different rhyme." Michael Boyle closed his account with a comparable observation. We will let P Flanagan continue:

"It started, you see, in different forms. There was different rhymes, you know, in different parts of the country.

"I told you the rhymes we had here, well, you may go to another district of the country and it might vary you see, and it mightn't just really be the same type of rhymes, but, of course, them all was connected with the mummers as far as that was. Them all came into meter just the same as I explained to you there.

"Some of them started off:

'The wran, the wran, the noble wran.
The king of all birds.
Although she's small, her family's great.
Rise up landlady and give us a trate.
If the trate is anyway big,
We'll make the wranboys dance a jig.
And if the trate is anyway small,
It'll not insult the wranboys all.
Here comes I that didn't come yet,
Big head, little wit.
Money I want, money I crave.
If you don't give me money,
I'll sweep yous all to your grave,
And bury the wran at your door.'

"That's the way they started off in some parts of the country. It went on like that.

"And then on the finish up then, he called the next member in from the door, you see, and the next follower would have a different rhyme, and that's the way it goes on. But really I don't know them all.

Geography: *A Custom in These Islands*

"They come in at the New Year. The New Year was their time.

"They might have an ensign with a bird, with a picture of a wran on it there, carryin it to show that they were the wrenboys.

"They had no natural bird. It wouldn't be easy, you know, gettin a wren; a wren is a very hard wee bird to catch. But they'd have often a wee bird on a picture there on a box. The money would go in that box.

"They were titled as the wrenboys, and they'd have this little bird up, you know, in front on a board, one on the box, and Miss Funny would go then, when the whole rhymes would be all gone through, the whole performance would be completed. She'd go forward then to you. If you were the occupant of the house, you gave your subscription to her then, your donation.

"That was that. And they'd leave peacefully."

The wrenboys' rhymes were learned by P from his father. They were recited by men through the hill country crossing the border of the Counties Cavan and Fermanagh, the area in which P's father was raised.

Many modern American folklorists seem little interested in comparative research. This is partially because they think hard-nosed social scientists are not either, and partially because of the enormity of their own nation. Almost any comparative speculations about American traditions have to be grounded on spotty, and often poor collecting. Great areas in America remain folkloristic unknown lands. The situation in Ireland is very different. There, folklore is an old interest among amateurs as well as professionals, and the island's two governments wisely provide funds for the collection of information on Irish traditions. The government of the Irish Republic established the Irish Folklore Commission in 1935 and its vast archive is now housed at the University of Dublin College at Belfield. There the notebooks of men who have collected in Fermanagh—good men like Michael J. Murphy and Alexander McConnell—can be examined. The Ulster Folk Museum, set up by the Northern Ireland Parliament in 1958, offers not only beautifully reconstructed examples of folk architecture, but as well a growing archive on dialect and oral literature.[3] I knew Fermanagh had been worked over less by folklorists than many other counties, so, with my American experience behind me, I was pleasantly surprised when I was able to locate the texts of several Fermanagh mummings, roughly contemporary with the play performed by Michael Boyle, P Flanagan, and friends.[4]

The territory claimed by the Ballymenone mummers was bounded on the east, south, and west by areas mummed by men who included the wren as one of their characters. Reports of wrenboy mummings come from Lisnaskea, east of Ballymenone across Upper Lough Erne, and from along an arc swinging from Knockninny, four miles south-southeast, through Kinawley, south-southwest, Killesher, southwest, to Florencecourt, four miles west-southwest of Ballymenone.[5] This tallies perfectly with P Flanagan's statement, for Kinawley in Fermanagh lies only two miles from the nearest point in County Cavan and P's father had lived near Kinawley.

Lads once processed with a wren and a rhyme after treats or money in parts of France and England and through all Ireland, save only the most northerly parts of Ulster. The acts and rhymes of wrenboy and mummer were so similar that they were smoothly meshed in many parts of Ireland, most notably in County Dublin and southwestern Ulster.[6] The Ballymenone mummers went out on the wrenboys' usual day, St. Stephen's, but their rhymes incorporated no bird.

The other texts of mummers' plays from Fermanagh are all different from the Ballymenone drama. The mummers of Belcoo and Boho, whose territory lay seven miles due west, began their play with speeches by the Captain and "Billsie Bob" that were nearly identical to those in Ballymenone, but their battle broke out between Prince George and Grand Turk or Green Knight rather than Saint Patrick, and neither Devil

Doubt nor Oliver Cromwell appeared on the scene. In an incompletely but engagingly described play from the Derry-gonnelly area, eleven miles to the northwest, Cromwell appears late in the "strawboys'" action, after Doctor Bighead has delivered a speech quite like Michael Boyle's. Travel another nine miles in the same direction will bring you to Garvary, near the western end of Lower Lough Erne, where the play has a Tom Funny in the opening procession and a battle between Cromwell and George; Divil Doubt is the collector and the only female character is a Lady who has no rhyme but dances with the Captain at the play's conclusion.[7]

The masterworks of drama, pickled in printer's ink, can survive to be performed, loved and misunderstood in inappropriate contexts. The same text for *Romeo and Juliet* might be used by a professional company in London's seventeenth century suburbs and by contemporary high school students in an Indiana gymnasium. A traditional play like the mumming, though, is constantly adjusted, balanced, and made new to keep it fitting its times and places. At Christmas in the 1930s there were three different teams operating in the nine mile stretch between Upper Lough Erne and the border at Belcoo. The texts of their mummings are easily distinguishable; each has a different victim.

No academy has a vested interest in the preservation of mumming. The mummers' play was their own to perform, modify, or forget. Their cultural identity lay partially in it. It was among their geographical signs: it helped them locate themselves, eliminating anomie and giving precision to the idea of "our district." Others in Ireland, in Britain, went out mumming, but no one else knew just their rhymes.

Performance:

Go in with a Vengeance

S OME ARTISTIC TRADITIONS are brittle. Their performers memorize and repeat. There is little margin in which the personality can be expressed, no built-in way for the performer to adapt his act for a specific audience. Others are like quicksand. Their performers are pushed naked into the spotlight and commanded to dance while the critic in the wings screams that they are not being original, then carps of arrogance if they do achieve a personal and novel statement.

Searching for alternatives to homegrown boredom, the artists and scholars of the end of the nineteenth century were carried into confrontation with a grand panoply of foreign arts and cultures. Contemplation of these experiences brought them the concept of relativism. By 1912, Kandinsky and the other artists of the *Blaue Reiter* had recognized that all traditions could produce equally valid artworks.[1] It is preposterous to evaluate a Bambara mask with respect to a portrait bust by Michelangelo. Both are superb. The anthropological expression of such thought holds all viable cultures to be equal. This modernist concept—relativism—is only beginning to be accepted by historians, art historians, and literary critics, but anthropologists, among whom the idea is over half a century old, are sensing some interior malaise about it all.[2] It is absurd (not to mention impossible) to keep one's life and research from flowing naturally together. If you cannot condemn head-hunting or grandmother-eating among foreign peoples, how can you condemn such folk activities as lynching in Louisiana or lying in Washington? Approval will follow explanation, and dispassionate objectivity will reinforce the status quo. Unswerving relativism is a political act and an absolute position. Relativism is a necessary intellectual exercise, I feel, but it is not an end in itself. It is a step toward good judgment.

One measure of an artistic tradition's goodness is the tolerance it allows its practitioners. Does it tyrannize over them so that creative individuals must reject it entirely? Does it prevent them from altering it to shape a more affectionate communication with their audiences? There are singers of ballads and operatic arias who do not feel free to change their songs' words or melodies to suit their own tastes; managers of television stations who will beam a show through to its end, though its audience has been numbed to sleep on the divan; children who will interrupt a story-telling friend, accusing him of making up, rather than repeating his tale; academicians who will snort, when faced with a colleague's mildly venturesome work, that it is interesting but not really folklore (or history or anthropology).

Within a tradition of the opposite kind, the artist is given so little direction that people of limited talent become afraid to participate and brilliant people burn their brains seeking some balance between plagiarism and confessional madness. Unaided by their critics, divorced from their audiences, modern artists must censor themselves rigorously, and there is no telling how many poets have destroyed good verse in fear for its reception or how many dramatists have been jailed in asylums for presenting their concepts a little too early or publicly. Art itself may benefit from a chaotic tradition, but for the sake of human beings, an artistic tradition should have rules comprehensible enough to let many perform, and rich enough to allow for constant, personal, and momentary variation.

The Ballymenone mumming was, I think, an admirably sane tradition. At one level of abstraction, Hugh Nolan could say it was "the same" as the play in Scotland, though Scots guisers on Hogmanay might enact Goloshan being killed by

Napoleon and revived by Doctor Gore.[3] At a shallower level
of abstraction lies the ideal concept of the local play, shared
by the Ballymenone mummers and different from that known
by other Fermanagh men. But, in reality each performance was
uniquely of its place and time because Michael Boyle, the
Flanagans, McBriens, and Quigleys could relate their performance sensitively to their own needs and immediate situations. To read their tradition's dimensions and virtues, we will
need to look closely at the limits of its variability, the rationale
of its performance. The variations I will describe now are not
those of different mummers but those of the same squad in
action.

St. Stephen's Day, Boxing Day, the Second Day of Christmas, was a major marker for the mummers. They might begin
then, or they might start out before Christmas and end then.
The more they mummed, the more ambitious they became.
In their last year, they started out before Christmas and continued past the Second Day. P Flanagan recalls:

"That time we went out thirteen rounds: twelve nights and
one day. Thirteen trips altogether.

"Our last day was New Year's Day, and we went out all
day long."

In daylight they took particular care with their costumes.
Miss Funny and the Doctor were attired realistically, their
costumes varying from year to year, depending upon the old
clothes they could collect. The others were dressed similarly,
one to the other. All wore a shirt of finical cotton. Prince
George's shirt simulated armor in being a pale hue: white or
yellow, silver or fawn. The other shirts could be any color:
blue, red, although they all had to be the same color and green
was preferred, being "the color of our own native land." Saint
Patrick's shirt hung below his knees, like a bishop's robe. The
other shirts were generally short, falling to a foot or so below
the waist. All were somewhat different in length, cut, and

workmanship, being, like the dress of Hardy's Wessex mummers, stitched mostly by the men's sisters or sweethearts.[4] They were made of two pieces of cotton cloth, sewn at the shoulders and sides. The shirts, thus, had no sleeves, except for that of the Captain. He made the first contact at the house's door, so it was important for his shirt to be well tailored. His sleeves were a sign of his leadership. They were gathered tightly at the wrists, blousing out above, ruffling in a bell below. The shirts were belted high with a straw rope or, more usually, with a sash, green again being the favored color.

At night, the Captain wore the same costume he did during the day, but the costumes of the others could be "rougher." They might dress differently on successive nights, as traveling through the countryside was hard on their clothing. Some would wear shirts like those worn in daylight, but no attempt was made to have the colors match. Others would wear a regular shirt, ideally "colored" (not white, that is), over their clothes. Most would at least have a sash on, but as P Flanagan remarked, "at night as long as you had your rhymes, you could just go out on your own." Some bedecked themselves elaborately; others chose not to.

The play transpired away from the hearth at the dark end of the kitchen. On a winter's night, even a person not in disguise is hard to recognize until he has taken a couple of steps away from the door toward the hearth. A carefully detailed costume could not have been noticed by the audience. From the angle of the drama, a suggestion of repetitious fantasy was sufficient. Still, the costumes had to reflect some care, as there were groups of men who would assemble a mumming team quickly and roam for a few hours after money to buy themselves drink. Their costuming was poor. To indicate that they were out mumming to mount a party for the entire community, as Michael Boyle and his comrades were, it was necessary for them, and particularly for their Captain, to be dressed well. P Flanagan said that people who were reluctant to admit them would often come to the door and peer out upon the mummers gathered on the street. Amazed or amused by the costumes, the householder would scratch his chin and then elect to let the play go on. The more houses, the more money: "It was well worth a lock of coppers in them days."

The costume's main component was the hat, worn night or day by all but the Doctor and Miss Funny. Each man crafted his own, so that each hat was different, and different each year, but all of them varied from a single model. Early on an icy gray morning, P Flanagan and I were sitting by the fire after our breakfast, drinking tea, smoking and talking about the mummers' hats. When, with amused exasperation, he realized that no verbal description would ever satisfy me, he sped outside and brought in an armload of rushes to demonstrate. Having played Miss Funny, P had never made a hat but he had watched often, "It's very easy makin a mummer's hat," he said.

You begin with a sally rod tied into a circle near thirteen inches in diameter. Bend a small handful of the longest oat straw over the hoop and divide it into three parts, two on one side, one on the other side of the hoop. Plait these, just as you would braid hair, and bind the "plat" at the end with twine. Make another plat next to the first, and another after that, until the hoop is full and the hat-to-be lies flat before you, the tied ends of each plat pointing outward like the rays in a child's drawing of the sun. Divide these into four bunches, bringing each one up, turning its end over and binding it down with green ribbon, so that atop the hat is a four-lobed dome; P likened it aptly to a crown. Leave a few of the longest straws standing erect. Some use wire or thin red and white twine to tie a green and yellow tassel made by their sisters to these straws. Others affix red-berried holly to them. Then, depending upon your taste, you might weave ribbons in and out of the straw plats and tie them into bows where they meet on the outside of the hat. Tinsel, too, may be woven through the hat and draped over the hoop. With your hat rising two and a half to three feet from your shoulders, you would have been seen

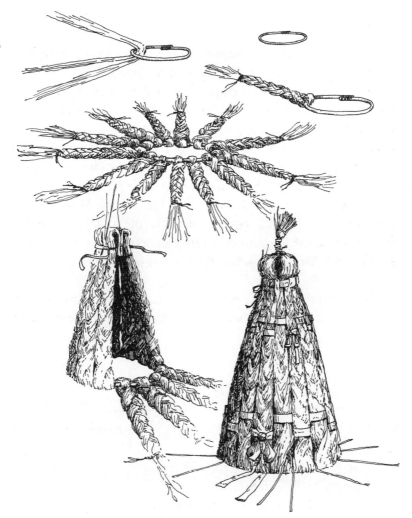

It's very easy makin a mummer's hat

at once as a mummer, as anonymous, as a representation of something not of this world.

During the days of planning before their first round, the costumes were made and the play was rehearsed. The text could be extensively varied to accommodate the number of men who wished to participate. On different nights of the same year, different numbers of men would show up to go out and even a man who arrived at the last minute could be given a part. As Michael Boyle described it, the play required eight "characters": the Captain, Beelzebub, Prince George, Oliver Cromwell, Saint Patrick, the Doctor, Big Head, and Miss Funny. Expansion was possible between the Doctor and Miss Funny. In addition to the lines for the eight characters who defined the play's norm, Mr. Boyle knew the rhymes for two others:

"One man was Jack Straw. He dressed in straw. All in straw. And a big straw helmet on him, same as the rest of us wore:

'Here comes I, Jack Straw.
If I don't get money, I must get law.'

"There was two ways of that rhyme. I heared it another way:

'Here comes I, Jack Straw.
With a stick in me hand ready to draw.
I had fourteen childer born in the one night and not two
    in the one town*land.'*

"That was the way of it. We used that rhyme first, but we thought it was too short and not long enough, and then we adopted that last one I told you, do y'see, to make it a bit longer.

"Well then, there was another character: Little Devil Doubt. She'd a besom. She was a lady.

'Here comes I Little Devil Doubt.
If I don't get money, I'll sweep yez all out.'

"He'd a besom. Twas made of heather. You seen heather in the bogs. Well, this heather was pulled and twas tied up in a wee bundle, do y'see: it was tied with a string and there was a long stick cut out of the hedge and it was stuck down into it. Oh, you could sweep the street or sweep the floor or anything with it.

"So, he was dressed up like a lady anyway. Same as Biddy Funny. And she came along and she said:

'Here comes I, Little Devil Doubt.
If I don't get money, I'll sweep yez all out.'

"She'd start to sweepin:

'Money I want.
Money I crave,
And if I don't get money, I'll sweep yez all to your grave.'

"That was Devil Doubt's rhyme. They'd come in sometime after the Doctor."

Mr. Boyle continued, noting that "you could leave out a character or two, if you hadn't the full cast." The first to be eliminated would be Jack Straw—his costume was a time consuming fabrication—and Little Devil Doubt, who was omitted because people occasionally objected to the violence of her lines.[5] If there were a player for Devil Doubt, he would not take his place in the procession when it was felt that his rhyme might offend or upset a house's inhabitants. For many performances, Little Devil Doubt would not be dressed as a woman, but would come costumed less distinctly in the usual shirt and straw hat.

P Flanagan also recalled some additional characters. At

least once they added a Prince Albert (a Victorian survival).
He had a vague memory, too, of a Grand Turk and a scrap of
his rhyme:

'Here comes I, Grand Turk.
From Turkey land I come.'

The Turk is George's usual antagonist in the plays of England
and eastern Ulster. P also remembered Devil Doubt:

'Here comes I, Little Devil Doubt.
If I don't get money, I'll sweep yez all out.'

And he remembered:

'Here I come Hector, Hector bold.
Hector: dog eater, man fighter.
And if you don't believe in what I say,
Enter in Miss Funny and she will clear the way.'[6]

Jack Straw, Devil Doubt, Hector and maybe others too,
could be inserted before Miss Funny, bringing the speaking
cast up to eleven or twelve, but the play was not enlarged endlessly. It had to be long enough to be worth a goodly donation,
but it had to be short enough to allow them to tour the max-
imum number of houses. So, there were also two dancers who
were costumed in shirts and straw hats but had no rhymes.
They were called in by the Captain at the drama's conclusion.
And there were the "followers"—young men who would
travel over the countryside with the mummers, watching to
see whether the performance went well, watching the treasury
grow. It would be their party too. They were participants but
their presence did not increase the play's length.

The play's plan set, off they would go. The excitement of
the new venture would get them in step to a tune, but soon
they would be straggling without music and chatting.[7] As a

forewarning they were noisy in their approach to each home. If they did not know the people of the house, they would put on the entire play, but if they did know them, they would stop for a conference. The houses of big spenders or attractive girls were hit with the full treatment. Their friends who had seen the play often before were given shorter presentations, as time might be spent after the play over tea. People known to be stingy, unfriendly or uninterested, were offered a still briefer "wee quickie."

During shortened performances, Jack Straw and Little Devil Doubt would stay out on the street. Either Prince George or Oliver Cromwell—Oliver generally—would be cut, the remaining English ruler being left to fight it out with Saint Patrick. Such a performance was described by Hugh Nolan. In a still more truncated presentation, like that described by P Flanagan, Saint Patrick would hang back with the followers and the ruction would break out between Prince George and Beelzebub. Another means for shortening the play was to leave the musician out of the procession. In the longer presentations, he would enter with a rhyme as Big Head; in shorter ones, the Captain would call him in after Miss Funny. The play could be put on with five characters: the Captain, Beelzebub, Prince George, the Doctor, and Miss Funny.

Coming across the texts offered by Hugh Nolan, Peter Flanagan, and Michael Boyle, a folklorist could suppose they represented different plays, or even different traditions, when actually they are different renditions of the same play. The contraction and expansion of the cast at different houses on the same night was enabled by the rhyme's identical ending couplet. It could be eliminated, any name could be plugged into it, and the players could number from five to a dozen.

The Captain knocked on the door with his walking stick and stood back politely. "Not everyone would admit them," Hugh Nolan said, "the young people liked them, the aged cranky people didn't want them." If the door cracked open, the Captain would consult with the householder. Some would say that they did not want the mummers to enter—there were sleeping children or sick people in the house—and they would give the mummers their "subscriptions" at the door.

If they were admitted, the tone of the performance would be altered, as P Flanagan remarked, "in accordance with the people of the house":

"If they were rough clients, they'd go in with a vengeance.

"But, if there was young children, the Captain would tell you to go in carefully. If there were young children there, you would take it coolly, afraid you would scare them.

"We had a code or rule. The Captain kept everyone just in order. If children were there, you would speak low.

"If children get excited, they would cause trouble for their parents. So they would."

They would enter the homes of small children quietly. If Little Devil Doubt came in, her rhyme would be given out in a "jokey" way so the children would know her threat was not serious. If the audience were unknown, the play would proceed with cool restraint. Known audiences, though, were treated to hot performances, flaring with violent actions and sputtering with impromptu additions. The battle would be stretched in time by wide gestures. The death could be accompanied by a gigantic yowl. The Captain's call for the Doctor might be echoed by other actors, and the Doctor might mutter, "I'm coming, I'm coming," as he hastened to the side of the slain man.

Usually the players would line up outside and enter, one by one, on cue. After long cold walks to the houses of people they knew well, like the Cutlers', they might all rush in at once and form a semicircle out of which each man would step as he delivered his speech.

The first act is Captain Mummer's. In most of the local homes, the front door gives into the kitchen at the end by the dresser, away from the fire. There are no pieces of furniture blocking the kitchen's middle. The two tables, one for dining, one for food preparation, stand next to the front and rear walls. The kitchen offers the mummers a natural stage. Projecting gentility, the Captain enters slowly and begins his rhymed request for room while walking toward the back of the kitchen, then circling toward the fire to mark out the arena. His rhyme ends after one revolution with him standing at the back of the kitchen. Each player says his piece while walking straight to his place in the line that curves from the Captain past the dresser toward the door. As the fight comes on, the combatants step out of the line and into the circle transcribed by the Captain. There they have their say and have it out. The Doctor enters, tips his hat as he introduces himself, and stands bent over the deceased to recite his lines. He goes down on one knee before mentioning his wonder-working elecampane, pulls the "dry bottle" from his trousers and tips it to the dead man's lips. Then, he flutters his hat up and down the length of the victim's body, while the dead man's legs jerk to show he is reviving. When he jumps up, the Doctor calls in the following character and they line up along the dresser.

If the musician enters as Big Head, he says his rhyme and takes his place in line. When Miss Funny comes in, some are ready for her. They beckon for her to receive their subscription. But normally, she gives her speech, falls into line, and the Captain calls out, "Give us a tune, Musician." The musician steps from the line or enters with the dancers, and the Captain asks for requests. If none are forthcoming, Big Head plays and the men dance a reel. If a reel were requested, it was usually "The Swallow's Tail," "The Heathery Breeze," "Floggin Reel," or "Murphy's Reel." Or the request might be for a jig, such as "The Irish Washerwoman" or "Haste to the Wedding."

Some might ask for a song. The most common request of the period was for "Kevin Barry." This ballad, still often sung in the pubs along the border, is a lament for an eighteen year old volunteer who was tortured and hung in 1920 for his part in a battle in Dublin streets which led to the deaths of two British soldiers.[8] Still, Protestants as well as Catholics called for it. Today, Catholics sing Orange songs and Protestants sing Fenian ones, but only in private situations where their musical expressions cannot be mistaken for political statements. But, as P Flanagan commented, after I had wondered aloud at the selection of "Kevin Barry," "There wasn't the same tension in Ireland that time." A Protestant who was evacuated from Belfast into the Fermanagh countryside during the Second World War (at about the time the mummers of Ballymenone were asking for requests) has left us a clear reminiscence in book form, which includes a good description of ceiliing. He was surprised that Catholics called at Protestant homes, surprised they sang their "rebel ballads" when they came, but he was haunted by their songs' "subtle beauty" and "tragic mood."[9] Rural Fermanagh was not, is not, Belfast. Neither was 1940, 1972. Nor is any song political propaganda only. W. B. Yeats felt the first stirrings of poecy in his breast when he read a book of Orange rhymes belonging to his grandmother's stable boy.[10]

The mummers' audience might also ask, as Reverend Lapham did, for the complete play to be repeated. P Flanagan:

"They might request for the whole performance to be done again. Some people was that interested, they might make the whole assembly go back out on the street and repeat the whole thing."

In some homes, then, the performance might consume time enough to put on five or six quickies in other houses. It was worth it, though, because well entertained householders could be expected to make a larger donation: "You could put the long arm on them."

When the dance had ended and the requests had been met, Miss Funny went forward to the "boss," the man whose family formed the farm's working core. If his donation were large, Miss Funny did not approach the others at the hearth, even if they were fumbling in their pockets for coin. If it were modest, she would approach each of the ceiliers and the grown or married men who were present, and often all but the children would drop a little something in her bag. It was at this point Miss Funny tendered invitations to the Mummers' Ball. Everyone who lived in the mummers' home locality was invited. Outside of the home district, people would be invited if they were originally from the area, so a few of the people met in Enniskillen were asked to come home for the Ball. Unknown people who gave generously or had especially attractive daughters were also invited. The girls would come, bringing their brothers, so the mummers' invitations brought new potential marriage partners into the community.

While P went around taking the collection, the kitchen was encircled by the players and their audience. One group began at Captain Mummer and curved, standing, costumed, past the dresser. The other began near his other shoulder and, standing

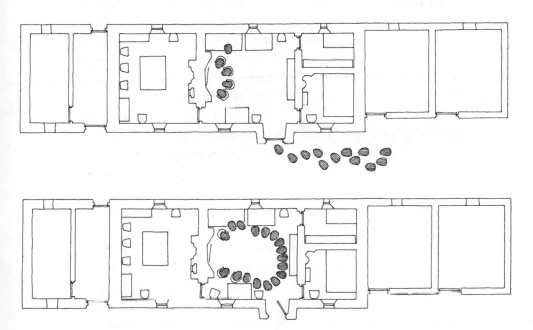

Plan of the play as integrating action

or sitting, arced past the hearth. Even the largest kitchen would be crowded and would provide for almost no distance between performer and audience. The audience became part of the performance.

I have heard the old ballads sung, the ancient tales told in small wooden houses in Southern Appalachian hollows. An old man will sit by the stove, his hands clenched on his knees, his eyes shut, straining to keep the sound full and tight, while his audience listens, attentive in tense silence, awaiting the release of the performer's conclusion. In Fermanagh it is different. The person who can stroke the conversation into monologue or tale is constantly encouraged by his hearers: "That's a holy terror," "You're right," "That's a sight," "Boys, o boys," "Man dear," "Now." The audience may join the singer in unison during the chorus or the last line of each stanza—exactly like William Morris imagined the followers of John Ball doing.[11] They will offer comments between many stanzas: "Manfully sung," "There's a rare air, now," "That's the boy can sing a song," "Good man." At least that comment—"Good man"—will follow the song's ending. The verb "to goodman" is locally synonymous with the verb to encourage. The singer or musician who is not "goodmanned" will soon lose heart. The mummers' audience did not sit quietly. Their laughter was great and loud. They felt free and nearly obligated to comment on the happenings, goodmanning each performer. One woman is remembered for her comical wish that her doctor were half so good as the one who rushed to the dead man's side.

The audience's role was not restricted to making informal responses. At the moment when the kitchen was circled, the participation of the audience members became formal. They were responsible for guessing the mummers' identities. An excellent book has been written on mumming as it persists in Newfoundland. There mummers at Christmas no longer recite rhymes, though once they did. Their event is made totally out of the confrontation of a disguised visitor and the householders who try to name him or her.[12] This aspect of the performance was not important in all of the Fermanagh houses the mummers played. Their costumes covered their identities and their voices were stylized to prevent recognition, but some people made no effort to name them and they passed out unknown. The last men out the door might lift their hats to give the inhabitants some clue as to who they were, or at least the neighborhood from which they hailed. But, if there were girls in the house, the stage was set for a frolic.

While the play went on, the girls would watch every motion closely. They held their guesses back until the time of the music and collection when they would shout names out. With a grand smile, P remembers:

"A girl, a young lassie, would shout, 'I know ye.'

"If you thought they were only just makin a guess, you'd try to pull back and leave them guessin. They would hear where the band was from, then, if they could recognize one member, they could guess the others.

"If they did identify you, then, well, most of them would take their hats off."

If their observations resulted in no identities, the girls would edge over toward the mummers, trying to peek through the less well-made hats, trying to trick them into speaking with their casual voices. Often a girl would pretend she had to fetch something from the dresser, a teacup perhaps, and sneak around behind them. Suddenly she would swoop to tear a mummer's hat off. The others would come to his rescue, tickling the girl, and a jovial battle would rage over the hat.

"There were times that the melee that ensued got that bad that the hat got bad abuse.

"That's a fact.

"Well, you couldn't hit a girl no matter what she'd do."

Laughing with the gay memory, P points out that the girls had a particular desire to guess who the mummers were, to become involved in the performance, because they were on the lookout for invitations to the Ball—and for husbands: "They'd be looking to the future. And as well lookin forward to the big mummers' dance. It was great."

The distance between the mummers and their audience began to decrease with Captain Mummer's rap. It further diminished through the requests and subscriptions, and was lost in the guessing tussle—a happy merging of audience and performer in a single act.

The men in the audience could also interact directly, physically with the mummers. The head of the household or his son might ask Miss Funny for a dance and whirl the floor with her to a waltz or polka played by the mummers' musician.

In many houses the mummers were offered tea and, at the Captain's discretion, the players might remove their hats and sit down with the family. In local terms this was a fair trans-action. Mumming, like music, like clever conversation, is called "entertainment." Food and drink, too, are termed "entertain-ment." The fiddler who entertains in a public house is set up with a drink, the ceilier who brings "entertainin chat" to the fireside is repaid in sweet, creamy tea and richly buttered bread. The mummers were often given edible entertainment by their audiences. And if the mummers were in a "rough" mood, what they stole from a house was not a silver spoon or a piece of crockery (though both were easily accessible on the dresser) but "entertainment"—things to eat. As he tells us in his excel-lent autobiography, Patrick Kavanagh, poet from the south Ulster County of Monaghan, went out with a hastily assembled mumming team to get money. From one house they filched bacon, from another a fruit cake.[13] This was not quite robbery. Remember Mrs. Cutler's well-wish to the bread stealing mum-mers. It was a trade of different sorts of entertainment.

Performance: *Go in with a Vengeance*

Whether it had been abrupt or full, restrained or wildly hilarious, the play ended in order as the men, their costumes readjusted, left one by one, wishing the house a happy Christmas. The young men of the house might choose to join the mummers' followers; P said, "Members of the family often came along with the mummers for miles, they found us so entertaining. And I think that's what kept the old tradition alive."

Though gone, the mummers were not forgotten. For weeks after their performance, said P Flanagan, young boys could be seen about the countryside playing mummer:

"Youngsters liked mumming. I seen youngsters at it, where they admired the mummers.

"Their fathers would have to make them the hats.

"They wouldn't go out and travel and make money. They had the wee game among themselves."

They were preparing in play to become the next group of rambling bachelors, the next generation of innovative mummers.

The progress of the mummers' performance may be broken into a series of scenes. In the first, the players perform without invitation. This is the drama. In the second, the players perform at the audience's request. This is the dance, song, or repetition of the drama. In the third, players and audience unite in the guessing game. In the fourth, the breakdown of the separation of performer and audience is complete and the reversal of roles begins as the audience entertains the players with food and drink. Reversal is complete in the fifth scene, when young boys play mummer on the hillside: the audience has become the players. This movement is an attack upon the Western tradition that separates an artist from his audience, a teacher from his class, a politician from his mob. The closed door was opened, the formal became informal, the unknown became known. The mummers attacked the forces that keep people apart.

Meaning:

The Performance of the Season

T HE WINTER NIGHT is not forgotten when you sit by a
Fermanagh hearth. The fire's glow melds with the light
of the oil lamp on the front table, but the kitchen's corners remain hidden in night. The fire is warm, but you must shift often
to move the chilled parts of your body around to face it. A
turf fire is quiet; it does not crack and pop: the winds over the
hills pound outside. Then in the wind, there is a sound on the
street. You listen and a moment later a tap comes to the door.
Excitement around the hearth will rise as you walk down the
kitchen, remove the board that stops drafts at the door's bottom, and swing it in for the Captain.

Let into the kitchen, the mummers were led into the mind.
Behind the eyes that followed Captain Mummer and all his
men, subtle and complicated connections were made. Not
everything that went on at a mumming could be sensed.
Thoughts were carried to the event covering it, suffusing it
with meaning.

Meanings have been studied less well than forms. Western
scholars are most comfortable when they study things with
limits, things they can control, and the matter of meanings
appears to be infinite and uncontrollable. Two people may
share the same syntax in a sentence, the same form in a folktale, but the semantics of the sentence, the meanings of the tale,
seem always to be different, personal, and idiosyncratic.

Since meanings vary without end and since so much of
meaning lies unavailable to scrutiny in the deep unconscious,
some scholars have studied forms and acts as if they were not ve-

hicles for meaning, limiting their work to orderly descriptions of sensate phenomena. To positivists of this kidney, an event like the mumming is only the sum of behaviors that can be captured on sound film. Others feel the only way out of the dilemma is to ignore the performer's intentions and the thoughts of the audience and to concentrate on the artwork as if meaning were immanent in its form. Such magicians often succeed only in forcing the artwork to reflect their own feelings.

The meaning of an artwork, its presence as a sign, is not to be found only in the thing itself, nor only in infinite personal associations. Meaning vibrates between these realities, between properties in the thing and ideas in the minds of its performers and audiences. The mummer might go out only because it is that time of year. He might be admitted only because he knocked. Ideas of this sort are too easy. They beg the question of meaning and shy away from the power of the unconscious. Not all young men went mumming; some people never admitted them. Mumming was a matter of choice, even if the rationale of the choice was stated only in the performance itself. Traditions are maintained largely for unconscious —known but unarticulated—reasons and if we are going to get beyond description to explanation, we will have to suppose a tradition's performers to be volitional, intelligent beings and we will have to take our task to be the clarification of the principles that give a tradition significance. Meaning, theoretically, fulfills the potential of the logic connecting all a thing is with all it can be.

We will find the meaning of mumming by entering the space between the people and their play and interpreting each in terms of the other. When I talked with people in Ballymenone, the drama was always related to its season. It would seem that one important face of the mumming semantic might be turned to view if we set the play back into its position in the year's cycle.

It took me awhile to figure out the year's divisions in the

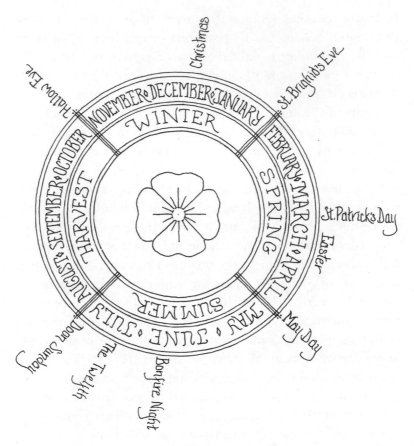

The Ballymenone year

Ballymenone countryside. People were used to translating their time into the seasonal patterns with which you and I were raised, but simultaneously their own year—"the old year"—turned in this manner: "spring" (also called "growth"): February, March, April; "summer": May, June, July; "harvest": August, September, October; "winter": November, December, January.

We might imagine potential Great Days at the points between each season and at each season's midpoint. Not all of these possibilities are locally exploited, however.

The first day of each season, the quarter day, was an

important marker in the traditional Irish calendar.[1] The strength of these days has faded into memory, but the memory retains hints of the controlling force a season's first day exerted over the period it began. It is still believed that whichever way the wind blows on Hallowe'en—generally called "Hallow Eve"—it will blow for the next three months. In 1973, in fact, the wind came out of the south on that day and it continued to do so through the ensuing traditional season of winter. On the Eve of St. Brighid's Day, the first of February, the first day of the traditional spring, crosses were woven of rushes.[2] Many of these crosses are still to be seen, inside near the entrances of some local houses and byres. On May Day, primroses were collected and tossed in the name of God from the home's front door. The thresholds and streets of a few local houses are still strewn with lovely wildflowers on the first day of the traditional summer. These, like the Brighid's crosses, insured a twelvemonth of luck. The last Sunday in July—the last before the season called harvest—was spent on Doon Mountain gathering berries. Harvest's first day, "Lammas," August first, is believed to begin three days of rain that leave the ground soggy, so that conditions are never perfect for the upcoming agricultural harvest. Winds, rains, and good luck, the conceptual forces of the quarter days reveal the now optimistic, now fatalistic, courageously realistic philosophy of Fermanagh country people.

Each season has one major celebration, but only one of these—Hallow Eve—lies on a seam joining one season to the next. The others arrive near the midpoints. According to Hugh Nolan, "Christmas and Easter and Hallow Eve were the principal Set Times—as we call them—in Fermanagh and the surrounding counties." Of nearly equal stature with these days was a festival falling near the middle of summer. For Catholics it was Midsummer's Eve, "Bonfire Night." For Protestants it was "The Twelfth" of July, the anniversary of the battle of the Boyne, where William III drowned the Jacobite hope in 1690.

St. Patrick's Day shared the middle of spring with Easter for Catholic people. Each was a Great Day and when they veered near their strength was redoubled. Said P Flanagan:

"When the palm and the shamrock meet, they said, Ireland will be free. That was an ould saying years and years ago. When Patrick's Day and Palm Sunday come on the one day.

"Well, that now happened six or seven years ago. Patrick's Day was a Sunday then. And we're still not free."

The Great Days are set into particular places in a yearly cycle of weather and light. At the same time, they are bound by similarities beyond sequences into a timeless logic of celebration. To this year, within this logic, mumming was complexly structured.

December is called "the Christmas month." With its first day, everyone begins to sense the oncoming excitement. Hugh Nolan outlines the period for us:

"From the beginning of December, all people look forward to Christmas.

"They communicate with their friends. Some communicate only at that time. They do send Christmas cards, the same as you sent me and I sent you.

"Christmas Eve it bes a great day for going out to towns.

"So then, on Christmas Day everyone goes to their places of worship: the Catholics go to the chapel and other denominations go to their churches.

"When the prayers are done, well then, they have the Christmas dinner. It's considered a great event. I'd be asked to some place on the afternoon. You would ceili on in the evening. So then on Christmas night you would generally be tired, and you would pass the night quietly in your own house.

"The Second Night, it bes a great night for dances and people enjoying themselves.

"Well, that continued until New Year's Day.

"In days gone by, there would be bands of fellows to gather up, maybe ten of a group. They would make hats. They were led by a Captain. And, as I told you before, the Captain would knock: 'Any admittance?'

"The Captain would come in and each man would be called in and he would have a rhyme to say. The performance ended up with a tune on the accordion or flute. So then, some two of the gang would dance. And they had this man dressed as a girl, do you see, and he had a wee tin box with a slit in it. We all slipped money in it.

"So then, they gathered up the money and had a dance in January with the money they got. They got some house or some hall. They would have a great supper. All the girls were invited. And anyone that paid would come."

"Midwinter" begins with the shortest, darkest days which are locally conceived to be those from the seventeenth to the twenty-second of December. Its core is "Christmas Week," running from Christmas Day through New Year's Day. By about December twenty-seventh the days' "turn" is seen. Light lingers longer into the evening, the days are brighter and clearer, and there is less low haze over the mountains forming the southwestern horizon. "Christmas" itself continues until "Old Christmas," the "Twelfth Day," the end of Midwinter.

The mummers began stirring with the shortest days, and usually before Old Christmas Night the year's greatest party —the Mummers' Ball—had taken place. Inside the party house were cigarettes, tea and cakes, a half barrel of stout. The older people talked, the younger ones danced; P Flanagan played the violin for many of those dances. And men would slip outside to drink the locally made poteen they had "joined" to buy and consume.

The mummers would divide up any cigarettes, food, or drink remaining at the party's demise. If money were left, they would invest it in a spree of their own within a few days. The men who had mummed would be traveling, too, to the balls put on by other mumming teams. P Flanagan recalls it all fondly:

"Ah now. It was the performance of the season. The real entertainin part of the year. The mummin and then the dance.

"And then after that Mummers' Ball, there might be a remnant of money that they might raise another wee dance on a smaller scale for the mummers themselves. Make it a second hoolie.

"And then, if there was another mummers' squad near at hand, well, they would ask the staff of our mummin to their party. Aye, it might be a continuation on through the twelve days of Christmas.

"They would keep on having parties. One would be linked up with the other, do you see. They were a kind of associated.

"They were very jovial times. They were. But now it's all over."

The twelve days of Christmas were, and still are, times of plentiful drink and constant ceiliing. The end of Midwinter was not, however, the end of the mummers' activities. Around St. Patrick's Day, the mummers gathered for a party. They built a great fire and in it burned their elaborate straw hats. The oat straw of the hats brought a memory of the past year's harvest into winter, and the hats carried a reminder of the winter celebration into spring.

The mummers' last party linked the main celebrations of winter, spring, and summer. St. Patrick, whose day in the middle of spring was chosen for the party, was killed and resurrected in the Midwinter play and was commemorated on Midsummer Night with bonfires like those which consumed the mummers' hats. The summer night that fell opposite the Mummers' Ball on the year's wheel provided the only party that rivaled the great mumming dance. Again, P Flanagan dips into his memory and paints us a warm picture:

"There used to be another great time here, as big as what the mummers' dance was. They called it Bonfire Night. It twas on the twenty–third of June. That used to be a great night too. Bonfire Night, they called it.

"It was supposed to be the night Saint Patrick landed in Ireland. On the twenty–third. And he lit the fire that never was quenched. That's the faith.

"It was even more common than what the mummin was really. You'd light a fire on your hillside. I'd light a fire here. And we'd sit around it. Maybe you're a neighbor. You'd come. All the neighbors round would come to that. And there would be another one lit maybe on another hill. Hilltops generally.

"And then it might be a whole communal or countryside fire. You'd bring a certain amount of turf out of your turf. I'd bring a certain amount of turf out of my turf. And maybe there might be twenty donkeys or twenty horses drawin, and we'd gather a stack of turf as big as this house, and bring a few gallons of oil and set them alight.

"And there'd gather maybe thousands of people to that fire. And they'd dance and sing and entertain—everyone was enjoyin themself. There would be entertainment now for everyone. There would be sing-song. There would be music. And that would go on from maybe six or eight in the evening till daylight in the morning.

"It was a wonderful time. Wonderful time altogether. It twould be very entertaining, and especially for the young people, you see. Aye.

"Young children, same as them children of yours, they'd be all assembled at it, you know, all assembled, and there would be all classes of songs sung and fairy tales told.

"You'd think you'd see the fairies—the wee folks—sittin on the branches just above you. It twould be generally at what they call a lone bush that they'd build this fire. That's a lonely bush, single outstanding. You often saw one growing in the middle of a field. And these fairy tales'd be told and the children would be lookin up in the bush to see the king of the fairies and his family.

"It was the greatest time of the year. And it was in such a good time of the year."

St. John's Eve, Midsummer, was a Catholic festivity. On the night before the Twelfth of July, the summer's major Protestant celebration, people gather at great leaping bonfires to chat and orate, make music and sing the old Orange songs.

Curtains are drawn tightly on long winter's nights, and the kitchen's window is blocked to prevent its light from spilling onto the street. Ceiliers on a starless night must pick their way through the dark silence with care. But at midnight on Christmas Eve a candle was placed in one or all the home's windows. "Some of the candles," Hugh Nolan said, "burned for six hours and a smaller one for about four hours. If the candle was a small one, it would be renewed. The idea was to give light to the wanderer." Mrs. Cutler noted that people would rise before dawn on Christmas and set up a new candle, if the one lit at midnight had burned down. Some let this candle flare until noon; others snuffed it at sunrise.

A scholar of a century past would race to connect these flames into a cycle of light. The modern scholar flinches at such thinking. His life passes in an artificial capsule. He is heated when it is cold, cooled when it is hot, lit when it is dark. The traditional Fermanagh house does not allow the luxury of such environmental alienation. Only a tiny minority of the people in Ballymenone and adjacent areas have electricity.[3] They know when the light fails each evening. During Midwinter, light is the ceili's first topic. Fermanagh people are deeply concerned with the annual ebb and flow of sunlight, and their concern is ancient: the precise orientations of the great gray stones heaving out of the British and Irish land-

scapes, standing in circles, lining the graves of forgotten war-
riors, prove that Midsummer and Midwinter have long been
Great Days. Whether it bothers my peers or not, it is true that
Ballymenone's happiest parties fell with daylight and darkness. A great fire burned away the black throughout the year's
shortest night. Through the long night at the opposite end of
the year, the night before the day on which the Light of the
World was born, candles sparkled along the lanes like earth-
thrown stars. And as soon as the days started to lengthen, a
drama was performed in which a dead man was brought back
to life. That man was the same who had brought light to Ireland on the year's longest day.

Having stumbled over a thought that seems suspiciously
survivalistic, we might take a look at an old Frazerian idea.
Today's dominant survivalists imagine the play to be the
wreckage of a life-cycle fertility ritual. An earlier idea was
that the death and rebirth in the mummers' play were magically
tied to the replacement of one year by another. Once, it is said,
people practiced the laudably sane custom of annually killing
their king and replacing him with a younger, more vigorous
leader to encourage the new year to spring up potently green.
The modern drama, the argument runs, is but a silly, secular
relic of this solemn ancient occasion. Now, if we ignore the
old assumption of degeneration, and replace the idea of magical
causation with one of logical relation and metaphoric involvement, the drama's connection to the death of one year and the
birth of another could be worth exploration.[4]

With regard to the play's suitability as a year ending en-
actment, it has been pointed out that the hearth's ashes must
not be removed on New Year's Day. Hence the appropriate-
ness of the threat of a broom-wielding Devil Doubt. There
might be a nutritious scrap in this porridge, for some people in
Ireland did believe it was bad luck to take the ashes out on New
Year's Day; they provided the house with continuity over a
fragile point. In Ballymenone, however, it was on May Day
that the house's ashes were not removed. P Flanagan said that

New Year's might be the correct day for the mummers' performance, but it was not their day. As is the case in many parts of Ireland, in Ballymenone the importance of New Year's Day is recent and slight. Only toward the end of their tenure did the mummers, realizing its importance for others, give it special attention. Bells clang in the new year in town, but January the first begins neither season nor year in the countryside. If the mummers went out in the spring, as they did in parts of England, or if New Year's Day had the importance it has in Scotland or the United States, it would be easier to relate the play's action to the arrival of a new year.[5] The Ballymenone drama is less clearly connected to another year than it is to the days' turn, the return of light, but the lengthening of the days signals the coming of spring, of growth, life and warmth—the beginning of another agricultural cycle.

Light flickers at the heart of Ballymenone's culture. The fire on the hearth burns in the middle of daily existence. The food on which life depends is cooked there. Children's games and adult conversations curl around it. The ancient märchen told children are called "fireside tales"; the ceili's talk is called "fireside chat"; the community's unwritten, yet formal laws pertaining to rights of land use and access are called "fireside law." The house with a cold hearth is considered dead: soon its thatch will fall, its walls will tumble. Chat by the fireside or roadside inevitably begins with the weather. It made sense for large gatherings to have fires at their centers and for the year's greatest parties to be balanced at climatic extremes. Those parties united the Great Days in their provision of entertainment.

The entertainments of the Great Days were those of the little days magnified. Workaday delights were enlarged.

Locally, "lonesome" means sad. The antisocial pleasures of reading or contemplative solitude are considered no pleasures at all. After my time in Ireland, the drama of Samuel Beckett opened up with startling clarity. Literary savants feel differently, but to me Beckett seems as Irish as his master, friend, and fellow Dubliner in Paris, James Joyce. *Waiting for Godot* appears before me as an immaculate negative of a normal interpersonal encounter on an Ulster country lane. Like Fermanagh men, Vladimir and Estragon stifle inner calls to hostility, cowardice, and madness by "passing the time": they talk, touch, and stay together, despite the hopelessness of their situation. In Fermanagh they say, "The man made time, made plenty." Time wears the will down. My friends in Ballymenone possess a stark, sharp awareness of their own existence.[6] "It is a world of troubles at the present time, and not a solution for them." But: "A man must live in all seasons." They break away from brooding, bravely assailing time in the search for entertainment. To be entertained you must be in society. The ceili of a few friends is the everyday pleasure. The Great Day is that much better, for you are out in a large crowd.

Any gathering's quality is gauged by things that pass the lips. Commonplace pleasure is taken in drinking the ceili's sweet tea. On one night, usually Sunday, most men hope to get out into larger company for a half-one of red wine or whiskey and several black bottles of Guinness' stout. The year's large occasions are times for still greater alcoholic intake. The ceili's tea is served up with buttered bread. On Sundays at least, meat —fowl or beef—is added to the daily dinner's potatoes and cabbage. The Great Days are marked by feasts. On Christmas, Mrs. Cutler said, the old people would fast until after the church service. Then came the Christmas dinner, the year's grandest feed. This Midwinter banquet is opened beyond the family, as the community makes certain that people living alone are invited to sit down to goose or turkey within the warmth of a large social setting. There are comparable large meals on the other Great Days. My family and I will not soon forget the best chicken we have ever tasted: it was an old cock who was sentenced, executed, baked over the Flanagans' turf smolder, and served up as the pièce de résistance of a sumptuous Hallow Eve dinner.

Not only were large meals eaten on all the Great Days, some of the foods were even the same. Boxty—a delicious concoction of mashed potato, pulped potato, and flour—was traditionally served first on Hallow Eve.[7] It might then be served throughout the three winter months, but at least it was served again on the Second Day, Boxing Day, from which P Flanagan supposed boxty took its name. Christmas, Hallow Eve, and St. Patrick's Day are made special by the presence of a fruit cake. Incidentally this shines a sidewise light on Saint Patrick's threat to chop his opponent up small as a fly and send him to the devil in a Christmas pie, because the fruit in the usual Christmas cake is currants, and flies could easily be mistaken for currants —a flicker of Senecan grotesquery.

While food and drink are poured in, words flow out. The "fireside chat" that deserves to be qualified as "entertainin" proceeds smoothly, undisrupted by silences that embarrass. "Say something!" Vladimir screams, pleads, in silence.[8] Good conversation runs along gaplessly, carrying new information or erupting in "turns"—unpredictable comical switches or surprisingly precise witticisms. The best of wit is formulated in couplets called "bids." Sunday night in the pub builds out of small talk, intensifies through "crack" into which "yarns" may be subtly set, and climaxes in ballads or instrumental music. Poetry and music are the perfect culmination of the verbal capacity.

Mumming was exceptional entertainment. Its excellence was molded and judged on the same principles that are used to distinguish the good fluter from the poor one, the "entertainin chatty man" from the "harmless, quiet wee man" and the "ould blether." The sound of the good musician or talker is full and unhalting, yet measured and clear. Both demonstrate their control in long, smooth runs. The speech of the mummers perfects these tendencies. Normally it marches in rhythm and rhyme, each word like each flute note is clear, but it breaks occasionally (as in the speeches of the Doctor and Jack Straw) into tumbling runs. The mummers' humor is an intensification of the ceili's wit: it is poetic and consists of turn upon turn. The Doctor's lines twist and whip, cracking absurdly.

The characters of the procession are turns in themselves. Why should Beelzebub be so self-satisfied and why should Hector proclaim himself dog-eater? It is funny: unexpected, yet coherent. Whatever else the mumming might be, it was an art, a powerfully compacted expression of a traditional aesthetic, an exacting test of the verbal, musical, and dancing abilities of its performers, and a fine entertainment for its audiences. Like the best of nights, the play ended in music. Music invites participation. The ballads in the pub involve more people than a conversation can, the fluter's notes will bring step dancers—old men and children—onto the bar's floor. Big Head's tune brings men without rhymes into the drama and prepares the household for the invitation to the Mummers' Ball where they can perform, in talk, song, and dance.

Drink, food, talk, music, these are "entertainment." And that, P Flanagan feels, is what most efficiently wired the Great Days together:

"There was no such thing in them days as goin away to town and gettin into lounge bars and drinkin all night. There might be an odd sup of drink at the Set Times: at Christmas, at Hallow Eve, and Easter. That would be the most of the drinking in them twelve months. Aye, Christmas, Hallowe'en, Easter, St. Patrick's Day, them was the Great Days.

"Entertainment wasn't very plentiful in them days, you know. Even the bonfire out on the hillside, it was just as entertainin. They were lookin forward to them wee bits of entertainment.

"There was a lot of bands, too, in them days. That was a great entertainment: march bands. Well, that was the out and out entertainment: maybe they beat once or twice a week.

"Well, that's the practice now in them days."

As P finishes, Joe adds:

"I mind one time up at Kinawley. I was out of the house one evenin. Troth, I heared the flute and the wee drum. I got out and follied them out the road.

"That was a bit of entertainment for me."

In the days of the mummers, there were four local fife and drum bands, three Catholic, one Protestant. Many of the young men belonged; Peter Flanagan did, so did Hugh Nolan. They practiced regularly, but their main performances lead us back to the Great Days. The Catholics paraded on St. Patrick's Day: P, who laughs that a flute should be emblazoned on his coat of arms, recalls that, "it would be the greatest day of their lives: Patrick's Day." For Protestants, it was the The Twelfth.

By Midsummer, Mrs. Cutler's orange lilies "blow out" to be ready for The Twelfth of July when a region's Orange Lodges assemble to troop in a town. In 1972, southwest Ulster's Lodges marched in Enniskillen: tramped under a banner ("God Save Our Queen"), strode through the town, down through the Hollow and up the Church Brae. Bands in Scots kilts, pipes wailing. Bands in white shirts, drums beating. "Scotland the Brave," "Inniskilling Dragoon," "Onward Christian Soldiers," they played from one bridge to the other and out onto a hillside for speeches. Lodge after Loyal Orange Lodge passed in review: country men, their faces scrubbed pink, marched by in black suits and Orange collarettes. Banners billowed in silk above them: "Fear God, Honour the King." There were scenes from the Williamite wars and pictures of Protestant martyrs and portraits of war heroes and visions of England giving the Bible to the world's darker races: "The Secret of England's Greatness." Bright images fluttered past. The street sides were lined with people, recognizing and greeting the marchers they knew, enjoying the drums and the color. At day's end, the pubs were crammed with men, drinking and singing.[9]

In their gowns of green, the mummers had marched up the same street at the year's other end. Trips away from home, public pleasures, and an extraordinarily expanded field for social interaction all distinguish the Great Days.

On the Great Days, the devices people use to separate themselves from each other break down. Entertainment crashes away from the fireside and out into the public. Uninvited, it comes to you, asking for attention, perhaps for loyalty, possibly for a gift. The Great Day enables requests that must normally be restrained. Consider P Flanagan's description of the spring celebration:

"Easter was celebrated by eating alot of eggs. They used to do that: eat maybe a dozen of eggs on Easter Sunday. Now they wouldn't eat as many.

"You wouldn't care about eating a dozen eggs.

"And they would empty the whole shells out and hang them on a bush. Some times they would push them over a branch. Sometimes they would put a string around them. Sometimes they would bore a wee hole and let a wee loopy lad through them.

"They would gleam in the sun, bright and white.

"It denoted good luck for the coming twelve months of the year: until Easter a year you'd have full and plenty. Sometimes the children would go out and throw them up and play with them and have the whole egg shells broke, and that was that.

"That was the way they celebrated Easter. It was an egg festival.

"I heard of King Farouk, king of Egypt; I heard tell of him eating every Easter a dozen of duck eggs and a goose egg. But there's no craze for eggs on people these days.

"And then of course there was puir people that wouldn't have any eggs. And I would save a big quantity to distribute to anyone that would come up to the door. You would give them eggs without any charge to make sure that everyone had sufficient eggs for Easter."

The gift of eggs was more than the provision of a day's

sustenance. It was the gift of "entertainment," for the eggs would become a special meal. And it was a social transaction.

Every ceilier in Ballymenone is offered food and drink. These gifts cannot be refused. If you are full and genuinely could not down another drop of tea (as I sometimes was) you must ask not to be asked, for once food is offered, it must be taken. One old man I had helped with his hay on a sunny afternoon, said, "I'd rather have you kick me in the teeth than not take tea with me." He was sincere; his tea solidified the bond that was developing between us.

The gifts of the Great Days are formal statements of alliance. With luck, the year's turf is won by Midsummer and you give an ass load—two creels—to the public hearth at which you gather in a mammoth open-air ceili to reaffirm your commitment to neighbors and friends. The eggs given at Easter, like the drink you set up in the public house at the Set Times and the meal you lay out for a lonely neighbor at Christmas, determine the relations between you and others.

Christmas is the time for gifts: parents who must discipline children give them toys and candy, children who have left the area send gifts home, shopkeepers give free groceries to their steady customers. Material objects are transferred to balance the emotional ledger, keeping the books clear for increasingly intense exchange. The formal request for assistance in farm work cannot be turned down any more than the formal request for Easter eggs or the formal offer of tea or liquor. The Christmas mummers ask for admittance to give you a play in which the Doctor gives his patient the gift of life. In turn, you give them money so they can buy food and drink to give you a party where you and the mummers will comingle, trading entertainment.

The denial of gifts also determined relations between people—negative relations. On May Day, if people come to the door with requests, they are turned away. Anything borrowed on May Day does not have to be repaid, and unpayable debts are socially disruptive. It was once believed that a successful

May Day borrower would be stealing a year's luck. Any milk taken away on that day would carry with it all the milk of the farm's cows for an entire twelve months. Even when this belief was no longer held, the person who came a-borrowing on May Day was viewed with suspicion. Still, some were willing to risk the name "witch" in hopes of gaining a year's luck or milk. Like the person who did not contribute turf to the bonfire or the person who refused to admit the mummers, the "witch" was willing to live in an area without being bound into the community by the proper public exchanges. The gifts of the Great Days established ties of mutual responsibility between people.[10]

The Great Day is associated with luck. The cross of St. Brighid's Day, the Easter egg tree, the flowers in the wind on May Day, all brought a year's luck, and the May Day borrower

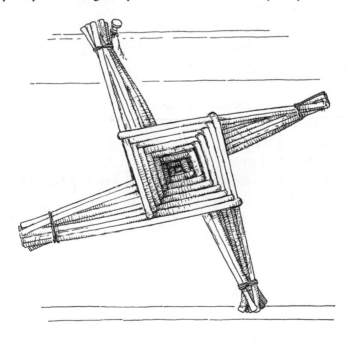

St. Brighid's cross over the door
of a South Fermanagh byre

tried to take it away. Scholars have often written that the mummers' task was to bring Christmastime luck to each house. I did not find this idea clearly articulated in Ballymenone, but hints of a connection were there. P Flanagan said that if the mumming wrenboys buried their wren at your door, you were in for a year of foul luck. As Mrs. Cutler remembered, the mummers who were refused admission cast sarcastic luck over both crop and beast. The idea was present in humor, and it did not seem to be stretching things past the breaking point to see the mummers' closing wish for a happy Christmas as incorporating a wish for a year of luck. Still, I was uncertain, so I wrote some letters off to Ireland, asking whether the mummers brought luck like the St. Brighid's cross. Mrs. Cutler wrote me back: "As regards mummers Yes and No. I never saw them bringing good or bad luck." Hugh Nolan responded at length:

"I am very glad to see that you are compiling this book on mumming. I am only too willing to give you any help in my power.

"As for the question in your letter I will try to answer to the best of my ability.

"As regard the people in the house, mumming was looked upon as a period of merryment especially where there were children. It was never looked upon as being a sign of good luck (or ill-luck) like St. Brigid's Cross.

"If the mummers were treated well, got a meal + got money they always wished the occupants of the house good luck.

"Their object on going out on this mission was to spend the money that they received in organizing a night's entertainment for the people that supported them. When their round of mumming was finished a night was appointed + a house was got for a dance + the money was spent on entertaining the guests. If any money remaining, it was spent on the children."

The mummers were not counted on to bring the house

luck, Mr. Nolan felt, but they did wish good luck to those who treated them well. Peter Flanagan was a mummer; he wrote:

"Just a few lines hoping you and family is getting along well for myself and Joe we are feeling fine. Well Henry you will have to excuse me for not answering your letter sooner but as you know it is the time for planting the potatoes and I forgot all about writing. We like to have some in case you and family would come to see us in the autumn. I often think I can see you coming across the hill. Well Henry to get down to the questions you want to know about mumming.

"Yes the mummers were supposed to bring good luck and if the occupants of the house were not Progressive it would increase their luck that the mummers would bestow a blessing upon them for the coming year and especially if they would subscribe generously to their fund."

"Here's luck" and "Here's health" are the usual toasts offered by Fermanagh drinkers. Luck in Ballymenone means "full and plenty"—prosperity. In a farming community, prosperity depends upon the health of the workers and their animals, upon the growth of plants. Luck is life. The dry snows of late winter and the cold winds of early March have passed by St. Patrick's Day. For luck, local people in the past would put something in the garden on the day or week—"Patrick's Week"—following St. Patrick's Day, though most of the garden would not go in until April. Patrick's color is the green of growing plants. His island, Ireland, is the emerald isle because even in winter life's green clothes the hills. On St. Patrick's Day people roved over the bogs in search of the dear little shamrock—"our national umbloom," Joyce punned it.[11] Today's skeptics may point out that it is always possible to find the shamrock growing, but some still believe that the green shamrock of St. Patrick's Day is the spring's first growth.

The theme of luck and life carried from the beginning of the season called "growth" through the natural year. The lucky egg tree was made by placing signs of life on a growing bush.[12] The flowers of May stood less obviously for life than eggs, yet they are comparable: the lucky flowers were scattered in the breezes, said P Flanagan, "to show that all nature is blooming forth at that time." On the last Sunday of summer, after the summer's bird, the cuckoo, has gone and salmon have appeared in the Arney River, natural fruits were gathered on the mountains in anticipation of the agricultural harvest. By October, the oats have been sheared and stooked, the main crop potatoes have been dug and built into rush covered heaps. There will be food for the winter. During the brightest of the two moons in that month, the Broc's Moon, the broc, the badger, wins the grasses he will store in the hedge for his winter's nourishment. On the last Sunday before the Christmas Month, Harvest Home was celebrated in chapel and church: large cabbages were brought in, turf was stacked down the aisle, and the ends of the pews were decorated with corn. In the dead of winter, for the full twelve days of Christmas, houses were decked with evergreen boughs and berried holly. Even those who have recently accepted the alien traditions of Christmas tree and poinsetta, continue to display green and blood-red vegetation at the time when nature is at her most grim. When the mummers entered the kitchen, their straw hats, manmade of dead "white" cultivated plantlife contrasted with the wild natural greenery which festooned the kitchen. The hats topped out in holly incorporated this opposition of life and death in a single artifact.

The Set Times focus on life and death. The year's growth is over when Hallow Eve fades into the Feast of the Dead. At Christmas, when the birth of Christ is celebrated, the mummers come with their act of young and act of age in which St. Patrick in his gown of green is killed and reborn. Easter is Resurrection.

The Great Days, as moments for life, as chances for social contract and integration, gear the year's cycle into the cycle of human life. They do so concretely. Among the barriers broken down at these times are those which prevent life, those separating men and women.

The night before the Day of the Dead, the first day of the old winter, was filled with thoughts of life. Death mocks life, but sexuality is rage against death. There is, in our tradition, an eerie harmony between the melodies of death and love. Iconographically, Death and Cupid are angels. The Christian at the peak of his love dies to be in the arms of his God. The poet at the peak of his desire "dies." On Hallow Eve, girls engaged in light-hearted divination. Fruit cakes, called "bracks," are still made for Hallowe'en with a ring baked into them. The girl whose slice includes the ring can expect to be married within the year. The activities of the young men bear intriguing comparison with those of the mummers.

On Hallow Eve, young unmarried men slipped up black lanes and rushed along hedges dressed as "strawboys." They wore regular hats, weirdly trimmed with ribbons and feathers. Their faces were blackened or hidden by homemade masks, and over their clothes rustled "mantles" of straw that hung plaited from a ring around their necks. Like the mummers, the strawboys were led by a Captain whose whispers controlled their movements. Protestant men did not roam out in strawboy guise, nor did strawboys go to the houses of Protestants. "They always kept on their own side," so that their behavior could not be misconstrued as political in intent.

As they traveled, the strawboys vented pent energies in pranks like removing cart wheels and lifting off gates and hiding them. Their objectives were the homes of unmarried girls. Into the kitchen they crashed: one man blew a flute or mouth organ, some danced with the girls of the house, the rest cavorted outside the norms of etiquette, demolishing the family's peace and stealing all the food in sight. These strawboys who traveled in large groups were tolerated. Barely tolerated. Similar restraint characterized the welcome extended to strawboys who appeared at weddings where their Captain would demand a dance with the bride. This was the last request the community of bachelors would make of the woman who was being taken from them.

Smaller groups of strawboys would also cross the hills in silence on Hallow Eve. These were led by a Captain who burned with a personal "spite" against someone. He would gather a few men around him to convince them of the justice in his anger. They would dress and strike quickly. They might tie the front door shut and stuff the chimney, filling the house with smoke and deep-staining soot, or they might "sod and stone" the doors and windows, likely smashing the latter. Usually such spite was held against people who kept their eligible daughters out of circulation.

Strawboys have appeared in the past few years. The tradition has not passed, although it has been hampered by the improvement of the roads over which police cars can speed into the back country. When the police could not get through the countryside with ease, though, the strawboys chose Hallow Eve to wander abroad like the spirits, to frolic with a house's young women, to attack those who held women from them, to batter violently at the conventions that frustrated sexual interchange.

The demeanor of the mummers was different. They wished to please the household to obtain a subscription to their dance. The mummers were, however, all bachelors, ranging in age from eighteen to thirty-five. When a man in Ballymenone married, he put mumming behind him. According to P Flanagan, the marriage of John McBrien, Captain Mummer, was the most immediate cause of the end of mumming:

"Ah, we had a good gang or staff of mummers. Then I don't know what happened to it. It died down, you know. I think it was due to the times mendin, you see, and plenty of money. It was a bit of hard work. It wasn't easy gettin around that time.

"And John McBrien got married. It wasn't that he had anything against it, but he just didn't have time for it. Of course, marriage changes everyone's life. But it was very entertainin in them days."

Disguised bachelors showed up at each house, but when they penetrated the warm kitchens of young women, their acts were most spirited and their play's aftermath most riotous. The mummers' play was the first act in a drama. It accelerated through interaction and ended with an invitation to further interaction. This offer was presented by a character, aptly named Funny, who embodied the merger of male and female principles: a man dressed as a woman. When playing Miss Funny, P said, "You posed as a girl and dressed as a girl, with hat and veil wig. She performed as best she could to entertain the people of the house, and the father or son would take Miss Funny out for a polka or waltz if he liked, and this was supposed to add to their luck, that some member of the family would get married in the coming year." The second act in the larger drama was set at the Ball where young men and women danced, moving rhythmically together in a pantomime of marriage. Mumming expanded the community's pool of marriageable people, uprooted the hedges dividing men and women, and cleared the way for the drama's climax: the wedding where the strawboys, the remaining single men, would demand their last dance.[13]

The mummers' play itself refers to this interaction. Without belaboring the sort of symbolism associated with the name of Sigmund Freud, we can note that the first character in the procession is Beelzebub, a jolly old man who bears a great club as well as a suggestively feminine dripping pan. The last character is Miss Funny who carries a leather bag. The procession includes a strawboy. Jack Straw is a characteristically Irish mumming figure. His rhyme in Ulster is often a riddle, the answer to which is a maggot, the worm of death.[14] When the Ballymenone mummers started out, his rhyme was:

'Here comes I Jack Straw,
If I don't get money I must get law.
Meal, flax, hemp or tow,
I must get money before I go.
If you don't believe in what I say,
Enter Little Devil Doubt and clear the way.'[15]

But the Ballymenone men invented him a new speech in which
he brandishes a stick and boasts of fathering fourteen children
in different townlands on the same night—a prodigious physical accomplishment.

The strawboys of Hallow Eve and the mummers of Christmas would once have looked more similar than they did in the
1930s. P Flanagan learned that in his father's day the mummers
were costumed in straw:

"Before our generation, I think, they were really all dressed
in straw. They were dressed more like th'Indians.

"They had a bandolier around them. And then there were
streamers hangin like these new–fashioned skirts now, you
know, them divided skirts, much like that. They'd have that
bandolier around their waist and these plats goin on down to,
well, below the knee.

"And they'd have their hood pulled over their heads, the
same as we did."

Bachelors in dresses of straw, who travel Hallow Eve with
the souls of the dead, who come out of winter's black nights,
promising fertility, return us symbolically, concretely to the
theme of life. The mummers keep death's company, but deny
its dominion. Death is the dying of the light, the onrush
of darkness. Light eliminates darkness. Light, as P Flanagan
told us, is the faith St. Patrick brought. Faith brings ever-
lasting life. The faithful are not tempted by the powers of
darkness, of ignorance and evil. They are not swept into a
grave of eternal darkness by the Devil of Doubt; they die to

ascend on wings to pure light. The year is at its darkest when the mummers begin. When they are finished light is on the increase. They have not caused but participated in a happy, natural transformation. In their drama, the Saint, despite his aura of greenness and light, is murdered by a worldly agent. Another agent, the Doctor, enters and gives a speech in which things by the hearth are treated as if they were animate—the besom has "spare ribs," the creepie stool has "livers and lights" or "thunder nouns" (wounds). The dead man is reborn, just as the faithful soul will be reborn after death. The Doctor's gift parallels the gift the mummers offer their community: in giving their play, they are playing their gift. The community is dying and without reproduction it will die. Their play displays their life–giving potential. Their request is that they be allowed to fulfill that potential.

The period after Christmas is a time for contracts. Land rentals on the "conacre" system—the "eleven month take"— are usually arranged then so that all will have enough land to work. Marriages are traditionally announced in the months after Christmas. These contracts insure prosperity and re-plenishment. Rather than waiting fatalistically, the young men force luck, asking for marriage partners so they can provide the community new members.

It is tempting for folklorists possessed of comparative in-formation to float superorganically above the realities of any particular community. We could gather ideas from elsewhere in Ireland and attach them to Ballymenone's year in order to reinforce the mumming's life-giving dimensions and possibly to resurrect the survivalists' view of mumming as a remnant of a fertility ritual. In some areas there were bonfires not only on St. Patrick's Day and Midsummer, but on Easter, May Day, the first day of harvest, and Hallowe'en as well. In some areas young men in disguises appeared on St. Brighid's Eve, Easter, and May Day as well as at Hallowe'en and Christmas, and men dressed in straw came to wrestle with living men at wakes as well as to dance with women at weddings.[16] It is easy to

The conquest of death
Details from the Auchenleck memorial of 1680
in the church at Bellanaleck

invent a clear scheme, and conceivably the year's events may have once been more similar, one to the other, and all may have been suffused with anxieties about fertility.

But the real mumming in a real community was ritualistically less exact than the survivalists might wish it to be. That does not mean it was poorer than the hypothetical mimes of ancient days. Less is more, the modern artists tell us.[17] With its uncluttered geometry and free semantic, the mumming of recent years was far richer than the phantom the old scholars envisioned. It cannot be reduced to a tool that served some single purpose. It exists in itself as an art, and like any art it presents without answering profound philosophical problems.

Like a rose, mumming unfolds to expose the inner logic of fundamental contraries: male and female, life and death, hope and despair. It does not dissolve ambiguity in clear resolution; in symbol and act, mumming has the power to ignite chain reactions of reference deep in its viewers' minds. For one person, the performance might suggest sexual interchange. Another could trip inwardly on ideas of social disjunction and contract, or faith, or politics, or aesthetics. Yet another might think outward through the Great Days, dismembering them and reordering their force along lines connecting light and luck with agricultural and human health. Its form, content, and location in the year throw broad limits around the meanings of mumming.[18] Its energies are those of human unity not discord, life not death, hope not despair. But by exposing the possibilities of discord, death, and despair it allows them too, much as Hamlet considers death's sweet sleep when rejecting suicide, or an outlaw ballad lets its hero take radical action against capitalistic oppressors before bringing him to the gallows. We might analyze the play in its annual setting and feel its essence to be the optimistic resolution of biological absolutes, but it is an art, not a science: it does not lie to people, pretending there are easy answers when there are not. If all ambiguity is removed, the play is only entertainment—an intensification of the very best in day in day out existence.

Function:

To Bring Unity amongst Them

O N A DRIZZLY DAY, I came up through the mud to pass a cigarette's moment with Tommy Love. A frequent ceilier at the Flanagans' and Hugh Nolan's, he leaned on his straight–snathed scythe while we smoked and talked of the weather. The conversation drifted to mumming and he offered me a sharp summary: "Mummers? That's a group of men who go from house to house getting money for drink."

Mr. Love's definition is precise. It leaps over art and performance to purpose: the goal of the mummers was money. Folklorists with their romantic dislike of the money economy, generally exile commerce from their concepts, and become upset when folk arts involve remunerative return. The scholars of mumming look upon the players' request for a shilling as a recent addition to the magical mime. It seems to them a degeneration of what was once a selfless luck-spreading act, comparable, perhaps, to the change in agricultural endeavor from the barter and communal work of the Middle Ages to the wage labor and agribusiness of modern times. Yet, the oldest full text of a mumming we have, the Revesby Play of 1779 from Lincolnshire, begins by asking "for bread and beer . . . And something out of your purse."[1] To see the play's connection to fertility demands interpretation that will remain forever fuzzy and open to attack. At best such thinking accounts for a few parts of the drama. But even a casual reading of the text shows that the drama's dynamic and its entire structure rely on the mummers' request. When Mrs. Cutler reconstituted the mummers' rhymes it was natural for her to conflate Beelzebub's opening statement with a closing demand for money. Similarly, P Flanagan meshed the opening speech and the request in his rendition of the wrenboy's rhymes. Their memories were less fragmentary than abstract.

The Captain enters, asking for room in which his followers will entertain you. He carries an ashplant or blackthorn stick, a prop for his gentlemanly swagger—and a famous local weapon. The next man carries a club, musket-like, over his shoulder and halts next to the Captain. The combatants march in with boasts of their warlike feats. One tells the other to pull out his purse and pay. He does not. A battle ensues and he is killed. The Doctor enters when he is offered ten pounds. He demands more than four times that amount. His demand is met. He wants no pay unless his medication works. It does, and he begins the call for the rest of the cast. Now, Big Head wishes to please you. But Hector vaunts like Oliver and George, the killers in the combat, proud of breaking the European taboo against dog-eating. In a local proverbial comparison, it is said that, "a man who would [do something dreadful], would eat dog." Jack Straw says in one of his rhymes that he carries a stick like Beelzebub; in the other he threatens you with a law-suit. Devils break into your house, the first after the Captain, the last before Miss Funny. The final two characters are both dressed as women, presenting an implicit threat to the solidarity of the male group and outright threats to you. If Little Devil Doubt gets no money, she will sweep you to your grave. If Miss Funny gets no money, she will steal your ass—the draft animal you depend on to get your milk to the creamery, your butter or turf to the town, to make a little cash.

Rhyme and action render it all humorous, but the words are clear. There are many young men, armed with sticks, standing around your kitchen who would like you to give them some money. The death of Saint Patrick shows you what happens to people who wrangle about purses—like that Miss Funny is placing in front of you—and his miraculous recovery shows you that paying could be beneficial to you.

The play's two processions are closely parallel. Each begins with a happy man—jolly Beelzebub, pleasing Big Head—who is followed by angry, threatening characters—Oliver Cromwell, Prince George, Saint Patrick; Hector, Jack Straw, Devil Doubt, Miss Funny. The first procession ends, then a fight ensues. Miss Funny ends the second procession but when she steps into line at the completion of her rhyme, the collection has not been made. The drama has not been resolved. There could be a second fight, and you are the logical victim. Instead, the Captain, who had called the Doctor in to save the slain man, calls two dancers in, thereby saving you. At the end of the first procession the angry words of two, differently attired men resulted in death. At the end of the second, the two men are dressed identically and they do not speak. There are no words to cause discord: they dance together in a demonstration of agreement. Some scholars, overconcerned with texts and inattentive to performance, have treated the dance as an appendage to the play. It is, in fact, the drama's denouement. Both halves of the play expose negative possibilities but conclude happily, first in Saint Patrick's resurrection and later with the dancers' reel. The mummers have used two, increasingly direct, means to suggest that it would be good to pay Miss Funny once the dancers are done.

Sometimes a simple statement of an act's obvious intentions seems sufficient. However, if the goal were only to get money, there would have been no reason for mumming. People who missed the play could still come to the house, give their subscription at the door, and sail into the Mummers' Ball. House parties were held without a mumming prologue. If the community needed capital to pay for road improvements or buy equipment for the bands, the word would get out, people would show up and contribute at the door. The Band Balls were among the great events of the past. Dances of the kind are still held in parochial halls to finance political activities. For some parties, termed "joins," an individual or a small group of men led by a treasurer (an uncostumed Miss Funny) would go about gathering money to purchase the necessary food and drink.

The mummers' goal was gathering money, but their purpose was grander than a full purse. Entertainment was part of this larger purpose. A coddled, dour lot, scholars always underestimate entertainment in their explanations of culture. For people whose days pass in rough work, an occasional break for enjoyment is not a trivial matter. Entertainment makes a hard life endurable. A Ballymenone saying puts it well: "A change is as good as a rest." What the mummers promised was exactly "divarsion."

Adding entertainment to shilling collecting still does not yield the full sum of the mummers' purpose. For a useful analogy, I will turn back to a conversation I had with my friend Johnnie Brendel, a few years before his death. When he was a child in a German speaking community of southeastern Pennsylvania, bizarrely garbed, masked figures called Belsnickels came to each house at Christmas. Their ostensive purpose was tossing pretzels, candy, and nuts to the children. At the same time, their antics brought entertainment to everyone in the household (for which they were repaid with drafts of hard cider). And quietly they acted in behalf of the whole community by chastizing bothersome children whose parents were lax in their discipline, and by giving food and clothing to poor people too proud to request or accept help from their neighbors.

In eastern Ulster a custom, apparently of Scottish origin, was practiced as an alternative to mumming. Young boys traipsed from house to house on New Year's Day, reciting a rhyme and distributing lucky wisps of braided straw in return for food, drink or money. On Rathlin Island, lying off County Antrim toward Scotland, these New Year's rhymers came blowing horns and trading bits of sheepskin for meal which they gave out then to the poor people of the Island.[2]

The Ballymenone mummers gained pleasure from their fraternity, the performance and party, but it was not pleasure alone that drove them. Under their event lay an unstated purpose, a communitarian consequence of the sort social scientists term functions. The Mummers' Rule directed them to knock on every door they came to. Their course would carry them on for several days, but they made a great effort to visit each house in their home community on one night, the first or last of their travels, so that all of the local people would hear of the Ball at once. During their first year many people were reluctant to admit them, being afraid to let masked men indoors, but the mummers returned carefully to those people every year, extending them the option of community involvement. The word got around that the mummers meant no harm, and eventually they were allowed to perform in most houses. At the play's end, even the older people who were unlikely to attend the party, would be expecting and would receive an invitation to the Ball.

Any community tends to fragment. Ballymenone people are "quiet" and "harmless" or they are "entertainin" and "full of sport." Networks of friendship based on personality and compatibility include some people and exclude others. Not everyone is of the same economic estate. The local ethic is genuinely egalitarian but people do classify each other as "big farmers," "small farmers" (in which category most workers fit), and landless "laborers." The wealthier farmers criticize the poorer ones for their lack of ambition; the poorer criticize the wealthier for sloppy practice and lack of self-sufficiency: with too many cows on too much land, the big farmers do not keep their hedges trim nor bother with gardens since they have money enough to buy the things the small farmers raise. In this sector of Ulster people are terribly divided by religious and political affiliations.

Ballymenone's traditional arts are mostly the province of the exceptional talent: the solo singer of ballads, the lone fiddler or fluter, the "star" teller of "yarns" and "rigamaroles." Mumming, however, invited broad participation in a group performance. There was a place for the extroverted and verbal man like Michael Boyle and a place, too, for a mild, taciturn man like Joe Flanagan.

Attendance at church or chapel might override natural friendship groupings and economic distinctions, but the Mummers' Ball was the only event in the area to which everyone was formally invited. Generally, all of the mummers were Catholics, though a few Protestants might travel along with them, but they went to Protestant homes as well as Catholic ones and acted with particular politeness at houses where they had heard they were not welcome.

Acting formally, decorously, as disguised impersonal characters, the mummers could move outside of the community's conventional distinctions to engage in a transaction with every person living in the area. The mummers contributed their energies, all others contributed their money. Miss Funny's collection was no cheap shot at capital gains. It was a joint venture in community strength, a monetarily sealed social contract.

As Samuel Beckett tells us through Molloy, anthropology has its fashions.[3] In Victorian England, when fundamentalist revivals, Catholic countermovements, and mystic spiritualism made for exciting tea-table topics, the survivalists reduced folk art to religion. In the 1920s and 1930s when functionalism was fashionable in the arts, most notably in architecture, it was also the rage in anthropology. Just as the Bauhaus designers tore the decorations from buildings to reveal their utilitarian functioning, the functionalists stripped cultures down to machines. Since the anthropologists of half a century ago were studying exotic societies that were flying apart under imperialistic pressure, it was reasonable for them to theorize that the pulleys and belts in those machines worked, like the organs in a body, to maintain the existence of the whole. A society's institutions, whether religious, political, or aesthetic were seen to exist to keep the society in balance. In trying to explain too much on one principle they, like the survivalists before them, explained too little. Certainly an art like mumming cannot be reduced to a component in a religious or a social mechanism.

Functionalism is now out of vogue. We are tired of crisp, anonymous office buildings and simple, circular schemes. But it is no more intelligent to consider an idea out of fashion than it is to consider one in fashion.[4] It is true that the Ballymenone mumming functioned to hold a fragmented community together.

Theory's purpose in the study of human beings is to improve our understanding of difficult problems through trial explanations that are never final but always in a state of becoming. Many of our most difficult and engaging problems arise because people act reasonably, but are not often fully conscious of how or why they do. Much of what they do well simply cannot be put into words, but there is also the possibility that, when presented with a theory explaining their behavior, it might jiggle the unconscious and enable them to bring known but unconsidered ideas into articulation, causing the latent to become manifest. I had gotten nowhere at all with casual questions about the play's connections to the new year or agricultural fertility, but one morning I explained functionalism to P Flanagan and asked him if he thought mumming helped hold the community together. He needed only an instant before responding:

"Aye surely. It was to bring unity amongst them and to show the opposite number that there was no harm in them.

"We would go to the houses of the people of Protestant persuasion and they were delighted. Often and often they would give more than what the Catholic people would.

"Some of the Protestants were confined like. They were a kind of strict and they loved to see a bit of entertainment like that. And when they would see the mummers, well, they were delighted with them, you know, and it changed their attitude altogether.

"Some of them would go to the Ball and they had a great time. Surely.

"It broke down alot of barriers. It changed public opinion altogether.

"If the mummin had spread—if people had become more mixed—it really wouldn't have developed as it has at the present time.

"I really think that."

P Flanagan's commentary is most perceptive. At the present time, bombs rock the towns, barricades block the country roads, suspicions and bad feelings keep neighbors apart. In the days of the mummers people got along better together. Mumming is now illegal and there is no chance for Catholics and Protestants to interact. Schools, sports—Catholics play Gaelic football, Protestants soccer—and bars are as religiously distinct as houses of worship.

With this deeper purpose for mumming in mind, let us turn back to the text of the play. In his fine book, *Irish Folk Drama*, Alan Gailey mentions an Ulster mumming troupe that showed Patrick defeating George in Catholic homes and William of Orange defeating James in Protestant homes.[5] They were willing to reinforce their community's traditional animosities. In the full Ballymenone play, Saint Patrick always lost. This outcome would seem most appropriate for Protestant audiences, but, in fact, the compromise was perfect. Saint Patrick loses but he has our sympathy: he is our surrogate in action. In many plays, George and Patrick are both saints. The situation is not unique to Ballymenone by any means, but here George is reduced to temporal status. Further, the Prince is a "bully" accompanied by militant, long-nosed Cromwell. Saint Patrick enters alone; Hugh Nolan remembered him as being unarmed. He loses but resiliently rises up "to fight again," calling to mind the lyrics of many rebel ballads in which Ireland's past defeats are admitted while her capacity for revival is extolled. The chorus of "Kevin Barry," the mummers' most common request, runs:

Another martyr for old Ireland,
Another murder for the crown.
Bad British laws may crush the Irish
But cannot keep their spirit down.

That ballad fit the play's political semantic neatly.

The logic of the combat in the Ballymenone mumming has a remarkable parallel in James Joyce's *Ulysses*. At the end of Book Two, in the Circe section, there is an accidently provoked verbal battle in which the names of St. George and St. Patrick, the colors orange and green, are evoked. Stephen, cast as Ireland's representative, is goaded to revenge by dead Irish heroes and by Ireland in her old woman personification. He is knocked down by a foul-mouthed, red-coated English soldier and lies as if dead until he is revived by Bloom. A man whose day and fantasies spin around death, sex, and biological realities, whose name is flower, Bloom has kept by the side of Stephen, the intellectual, because he has Stephen's money.

From the time of his boyhood, James Joyce loved drama, he acted in plays, and he could have seen mummings near Dublin. Another look at his novel will bring us closer to the associations between our play and his book. Earlier in the day, Stephen and his friends (autobiographically they are Joyce and his friends, the group Joyce called "the mummers") are talking about drama. Buck calls Stephen a "mournful mummer," for he is wearing black and brooding over the death of his mother. Buck says he has "conceived a play for the mummers" which will involve them with prostitutes. As they are parting, a man steps between them, and a first, fleeting contact is made between Stephen and Bloom. That night's scene is set up like a play and does carry them into a house of prostitution. In Nighttown, Bloom has a vision in which he is crowned king of Ireland: his procession includes Bloom's Boys who come chanting the wrenboys' rhyme. The wrenboys' day is St. Stephen's Day and from *A Portrait of the Artist as a Young Man* we know Stephen identified with his namesake, the Church's first martyr. The way is prepared for Stephen to become Bloom's boy, his son, and Ireland's martyr.[6]

Up to this point much of the power of *Ulysses* has been generated out of the opposition of Stephen and Bloom. In this scene, the book's climax, they are moved together, so that their differences can be resolved, so that Bloom can become parent to the boy. Both figuratively die to be reborn and both have hallucinations of dead family members—Stephen of his mother, Bloom of his son. Once Stephen revives, quoting Yeats, Stephen and Bloom stay together, each compensating the other for his loss and lack. Both men are expressions of one psyche—Joyce's. Early in the day, they wander independently as a schizophrenic projection. At night, through separate identification with Ireland (their spatial reality) and recognition of death (their temporal reality), they arrive at a cooperative relationship, and the spirit of the novel and the psyche of its author heave tenderly toward love, maturity, and union.[7]

It matters little whether James Joyce intended the Night-town drama to parallel a mumming. What is important is that there are deep logical affinities between them, and between them and *Finnegans Wake*. In the *Wake*, the Great Days, especially New Year and Christmas ("youlldied"), are exposed as moments for death and life. Battles sputter through it, pitting the green Catholic South against the black Protestant North, Saint Patrick against the "orangetawneymen" and "the bester of the boyne," the Irish against the English: "For Ehren, boys, gobrawl."

Lots are the puns on mumming in *Finnegans Wake*.[8] Mumming is tied to murmuring, mysterious, artistic speech. The Doctor's charm is "murmury." The wrenboys' rhyme crops up often; at one point it becomes "the rann, the rann, that keen of old bards." The mummers are entertaining; they are "whimsicalissimo." Early in the book, mumming is connected with Irish political divisions, with religious and military conflict, but later the mummers emerge among the forces for life and unity. In puns crossing mum and mom, they become female as well as male life-givers. With Giordano Bruno, they are "genitalmen from Veruno"—potent aids in the achievement of a single truth. Bruno the Nolan, a constant philosophical guide of Joyce's, theorizes worldly confusions in terms of dichotomies that dissolve in ultimate unity. Death and life are not an unresolvable antinomy, and the whole wonderful book pulsates biologically, spiritually, in cycles of falling and rising, dying and rebirth. Humpty Dumpty falls and all the English king's materialistic, beer drinking men cannot get him back together again. But "all the Queen's Mum" can perform a "Mumtiplay" to help him reintegrate and merge with his opposite, Tim Finnegan, sweet-tongued tippler of the Irish comical ballad, "Finnegan's Wake," who falls from a ladder and apparently dies, only to be revived when liquor spills over him at his wake. Doubling, cleaving, wakening, waked, the *Wake* is the savage mind in which combat becomes love, love combat, and diversity is unified in order to endure as diversity.

In mumming and in the magnificent novels of James Joyce, deep divisions are concretized in Irish political imagery, death is conquered by love, by rebirth enabling social and mental integration. Joyce, like the mummers, speaks for life.

The relationships between folklore and belles lettres have been weakly examined. Scholars have emphasized the obvious differences between oral and written arts rather than using their profound similarities to illumine humanity. During the 1930s, Joyce was living away from Ireland, writing the most venturesome, ambitious work in the English language. At the same time, P Flanagan and his friends were performing a conservative and modest drama in Irish country kitchens. Their media were different but their works grew from the same conceptual matrix, exposing the anxieties and hopes they shared as men and Irishmen.

Function: *To Bring Unity amongst Them*

The divisions of the Irish community—Joyce's Dublin or Flanagan's Ballymenone—are personified in Saint Patrick and Prince George. The political tensions obtaining between Ireland and England (a George wore England's crown at the time), effectively represented all the community's potential for hostile confrontation. Political oppositions are used in the Ballymenone drama as sociocultural oppositions are in Indonesian ludruk theater,[9] as the myriad opposed pairs of characters and traits are in *Finnegans Wake*: they bring the pure idea of conflict to the surface as believable dissonance.

Dramatic action and social action face each other like mirrors across a hall. The dramatic arts employ social realities to gain admittance to the kitchen of consciousness. Social arts use dramatic action to explore the perimeters of the possible. Drama requires conflict: there must be tension between Doctor Faustus and Mephistophilis, between Krapp the recorder, Krapp the listener, between Saint Patrick and Prince George or there will be no play. Social action will result in conflict and conflict will have its victor, its victim. Saint Patrick loses, as Ireland has, as every person will in some social interaction, but the victim reappears as the conqueror of death.[10] Action—social being—kills death.

In one of its simultaneous incarnations, mumming is a symbolic essay on the drama of social interchange. Our understanding of the play's dramatis personae will be helped if we look at the way the people of Ballymenone conceptualize their own actions. They array them along a spectrum in accordance with the pleasures they bring to the individual and the dangers they bring to others. "Boredom" smothers the person who has neither work nor company. An activity is not bad (though neither is it "good") if it "passes the time," as work, odd hobbies, and uneventful small talk do. "Entertainment" is a happy "harmless" interaction. Conceptually overlapping with "entertainment" but edging away from it toward the brink of danger is "sport." Sport is the name for the strawboys' rough pranks, for the aggressive twitting called "codding," for drinking to joyous excess, for the rugged, thumping Gaelic football matches that occupy stage center of the Feast of the Assumption on August 15 at "The Sport at Belcoo" in southwestern Fermanagh. "Sport" stretches from "entertainment" toward "fight." In the old days, factions fought with ashplants at fairs, and neighbors battled with fists and lawyers over "mearns and passes"—niggling matters of trespass. Codding can still lead to punches, and political speeches to bombs and bloodshed.

The boastful, weakly motivated fight in the drama is the kind people have seen. It is followed by characters who play between "entertainment" and "sport" and sally through codding toward "fight." Sitting at the hearth, you are threatened nearly as openly as the English Prince and Irish Saint menaced each other. The drama honestly displays the community's genuine potential for violence, but it contains it, subdues it, resolving its tensions in "entertainment," in music and dance.

Midwinter is bitter, dark. After having given less than eight hours of low, raking light, the sun has gone before five o'clock and the wet winds have risen. "It is the black, the really bad time of year," a natural time for retreat, suspicion, and unneighborly anger. Pay the mummers and you will have formed a bond with them like that which connected Stephen and Bloom, Patrick and the Doctor. The Doctor, the healer, is the spirit of the mummers. Pay them, and you will have invested in a party where you can be brought back to community life, no matter what divisive troubles may lie in the past.

Let us stop for a summary. Suppose that mumming began before the Christian era and that its original function was to insure agricultural fertility, just as the survivalists have argued. The broad geographical distribution of mumming suggests a great depth in time, and there are recorded instances—in Gautemala, for example[11]—of pagan rituals merging with Christian celebrations, then changing into secular performances. Fertility as a dimension of luck, as the climax of courtship, does exist in mumming's semantic field, but the play's modern function was not fertility magic. This does not mean the play was a purposeless survival: its functions changed to entertainment and the encouragement of community feelings. For people who work hard, who live together but who are kept apart by personality, faith, and politics, those are neither trivial nor degenerate needs.

The functions of the Ballymenone play provide the key to its recent history. The play was part of the community's life. The community was affected by international political and economic happenings. The play fared with the community.

Whatever its ultimate origins, it seems likely that when Englishmen and Scots colonized Ulster in the seventeenth century, they brought their mummings with them. The English battle between St. George and the Turkey Champion had medieval, anti-Islamic, religious overtones which eased the play's adaptation to the Irish religious situation. Saint Patrick took up where the Turk left off and often in the west of Ulster became the battle's victor.

Mumming throve in the Ulster climate. This was not because it was ancient. The answer to the question of survival, of historic continuity, has nothing to do with age. Modern mumming revivals generally fail,[12] even though the play is old. Tradition is not an explanation. The play was given a home in Fermanagh because it bore similarities to Irish traditions like the wrenboys' procession, because it could be fitted into the contemporary culture. Mumming was molded to become responsive in terms of the local semantic, to be useful in terms of local needs and wishes. Reinforced by the publication of chapbooks containing the play's text,[13] mumming was a common delight in nineteenth century Fermanagh. But it was outlawed and killed off during the period of violence between the Easter Rising of 1916 and the Civil War of 1922.[14]

Peace came slowly. Southern Fermanagh with its Catholic Nationalist majority, was one of the disputed areas with which the Border Commission was supposed to deal. The unease of the times kept Protestants and Catholics apart and split the Catholics into two abrasive camps. Some were Sinn Feiners, rebels who supported de Valera in opposition to partition. Others were Molly Maguires who hoped the border would bring peace at last. Ballymenone was ripped, its Catholic fluters and drummers split into two bands. In this context an elderly man, James Owens, decided to revive mumming. Like Hugh Nolan, the great changes he had witnessed developed within him a clear historical consciousness. He had made a great effort to preserve a mental record of past traditions. After knowing me for a while, P Flanagan pronounced Owens a folklorist.

James Owens remembered the mummers' rhymes from before the Troubles and he was friends with young John Mc-Brien. With Peter Cassidy, a respected intellect and noted performer of comical songs, they gathered the young men of the locality together. Almost all were Fenian sympathizers, almost all came from three townlands in Ballymenone. A circle a quarter of a mile in diameter drawn on a map would ring most of their homes. Having been raised during the Troubles, none of the new mummers knew any rhymes, so Owens wrote their parts out for them. Folklorists seem to dislike writing, but songs in southern Fermanagh are normally transmitted on hand-written pages. The people are quite literate and they have great respect for the poet's craft; it is important, they feel, to have the words right.

In addition to the rhymes, James Owens and Peter Cassidy gave the young men the Mummers' Rule requiring obedience to the Captain, politeness, and a visit to every house. James Owens and Peter Cassidy intelligently diagnosed their community's ills and prescribed a cure. They recognized mumming's functional potential. Their motive—the play's function—was not to maintain balance in an isolated community, but to bring balance to a community torn between nations at war. They responded to their potential as leaders of young men and acted responsibly toward their little community, harnessing an old tradition to a new task. It was a small but successful revitalization movement. Mumming seems actually to have helped in making the period between the world wars one that everyone remembers as a relaxed, peaceful time.

For over a decade, the young men gathered before Christmas, practiced and trekked to each house, providing all with an opportunity to become active members of the community. Their own sense of comradeship was enhanced at the same time. The immediate entertainment, the feelings of fraternity and community, made lovely memories that are occasionally brought out with pleasure and turned over for better examination. I did not study my friends, we sat together and studied a tradition they knew to be significant.

Again the tradition expired. The immediate causes were the wedding of Captain Mummer and the restoration of governmental restrictions during World War II. Having to go before a policeman to apply for a permit for the band to parade, or the players to mum, knocked an edge off the delights that once spilled spontaneously out of the countryside. Neither the mummers nor their audiences, however, are satisfied with such simple explanations of the tradition's death.

Tommy Lunny, a slyly witty man, a neighbor of Mrs. Cutler's and a regular ceilier at the Flanagans', went out with the mummers. He does not, though, remember any of the rhymes. The older people, he says, share sweet memories of mumming, but it is gone now, replaced by newer activities.

"Old people do always say that the weather was better, all things were better when they were young, but the young people have different ways.

"The young become old. Then they look back on their ways as best. And so it goes.

"Things are forgotten. There's no more mummin. Things go on."

Michael J. Murphy, playwright and folklorist from the south Ulster County of Armagh, went mumming as a young man and his explanation for the tradition's failing is the same: mumming is not sophisticated enough to interest today's young people.[15] This is quite a modern theory. The idea is that each generation has needs, and, though they are expressed differently, they are met nonetheless. Behaviorally oriented historians, anthropologists, and folklorists all often offer notions of this sort. Modern folklorists chastize their elders for weeping over the graves of the ancient genres of folk art. Vibrant new genres, such as the joke, they say, replace weary old ones like the märchen. Actually new jokes replace old jokes and nothing fills the need the old stories did. Television does supply repetitive fantasy, but there is no contact between the audience and the television actor, and should a person incline to performance, there is little for him to do except exploit the short forms he has always had and stifle his larger desires for creative communication. Obviously, a nation can have fewer television stars than master storytellers. Each generation does have its own ways, but for real people, change does not bring an endless sequence of identical possibilities. Nothing replaced mumming. The human needs it filled are no longer being met.

"Up in the State," P Flanagan says, "the mummers still go out, but down here in the North, money has got too plentiful." That is the reason he and Hugh Nolan give to explain why the next generation of young men did not take up where they left off. The young men feel a need for capital. They take jobs that hold them away from their community during most of their waking hours. They buy cars to travel great distances to events at which they are spectators. They buy electrical devices to provide themselves with entertainment. Mumming does not fit their culture.

In England, the geographical distribution of mumming correlates with the distribution of openfield villages in which people lived closely together and worked cooperatively. With very few exceptions, neither the openfield village nor mumming took root in the United States. The American settlers left cooperative villages and art forms behind them when they ripped into the New World's wilderness, but on the American landscape people live apart, work alone, and their traditional arts are individual expressions.[16]

In Ballymenone, farmhouses are sited separately, but by American standards the farms are small, the roads are numerous, and any view over the open landscape takes in many houses. The bogs and moss ground are shared so that even a man digging alone is working within calling distance of his neighbors. In the days of the mummers, people worked together in the bogs and meadows. Men "joined" to share beasts and equipment as well as drink. A "methal of men" could be easily gathered to work the farm of a sick man or widow, or to help a neighbor in need. If the river flowed over the bottoms a methal would collect to save the hay. If a house burned, a methal would have it rebuilt and thatched in a week.[17] Mumming was built on the same ethical frame as the methal: it depended on the ability of men to cooperate for the community's good. P Flanagan feels that since mumming has been revived in the past, it could be revived again, though it would be difficult, he says, because the young men do not know the rhymes. More importantly, they have lost the communal ethic.

The mumming memory reflects upon a time when the community was still a concern of its members. The nostalgia for mumming is not only bereavement for a dead art. It is a lament for an art that represented a lifeway. Mumming was not one generation's fad. It was the expression of a system of values that endured for centuries and has only recently failed. When we look at mumming, we are examining the way a communal logic works. When we study its functions, we are exposing and explicating the virtues of collective action.

You and I are readers, observers more than actors, consumers more than producers of entertainment. We can understand why the young men of Fermanagh no longer go slogging through bad winter nights to act out a comical play in the houses of people they do not know and may even dislike. Like us, they enjoy the comforts of self-centered existence. But we are beginning to realize that these selfish pleasures can snap back at us in criminal violence, in environmental waste, in mental illness. Perhaps we can also understand why the mummers once marched through the chilly nights, and why the old mummer is angry.

"Ah now. Nice harmless sport like the mummin is great. It is very entertaining. Youngsters wouldn't ask better than that. They would like it as well as a cinema. Open daylight sport like that. They'd appreciate it very much. So they would.

"It would be a great thing yet. But you can't get the young people now to do things like that.

"The people has got too old-fashioned to learn things like that now anyway.

"Sure, the fellows goin now are no good at all. They're not worth talking about."

Betrayed by the future the scientists promised, lost in alienation, we have a deep need to understand people whose sense of community was strong enough to allow personal deviation and contain aggression, whose sense of community required them to push out into personal contact with everyone in their neighborhood. In Ballymenone, the communal ethic is a vivid memory and a continuing reality for the older people who work and ceili together. But only the individualistic folk arts like ballad singing still flourish. The cooperative methal, the public gathering by the bonfire, the group performances of the mummers are gone.

Christmas remains a time for contact. Ceiliing steps up, Christmas cards are sent out, family members return from their labor in the cities to visit their homes. Our alienation is incomplete. Some of us have given up, curled up like the vanquished in Samuel Beckett's *The Lost Ones*. Others of us survive our boredom only by dint of private projects, lying alone, dying, like Malone in bed writing his story of a sojourn among the peasants. Most of us, like Winnie in *Happy Days*, like Vladimir in

Doin the town

Godot, cling to family and friends.[18] But we have given up on community. Without community we are vulnerable to manipulation as interchangeable parts in a system scaled beyond our ken or control. There is nothing to prevent the momentum of competitive self-indulgence from carrying us past comfort to isolation and despair on a blasted landscape. The philosopher, James Owens, armed the mummers and put them on the road in a resistance movement against modern times.

The last day Michael Boyle, P Flanagan, and their friends went out, they secured a permit and hired a lorry to take them to Enniskillen. They performed at the Imperial Hotel, P said, and all along the town's streets.

"We done the whole town. We went up the main street and out to Portora. The college boys nearly tore us asunder. They were that glad to see us. The headmaster gave us ten shillings.

"They were so delighted."

It is one of history's little turns that the mummers' last performance was at Portora Royal School—Samuel Beckett's school. Beckett shares with the mummers an ability to spark laughter in the brain's forbidden caves. But Beckett and the mummers are most alike in advocating the human will in terms suiting their own very different contexts. Beckett, the dramatist, the novelist, is the finest ethnographer of post-modern existence. He takes us down to the desolate, down to the empty, stricken floor of our reality, where we see lonely, prone, ill and impotent men who maintain the courage to live without hope. The mummers arrived at the gates of his school as ambassadors from a strange land and past time. Spokesmen for communal goodwill, their anachronistic message was hope.

ENVOI

Fare Thee Well for a While

1974

IT IS THE NIGHT after the first day of the new year. I lie in the small, low-ceiled bedroom off the lower end of the Flanagans' kitchen. The bed clothes are mounded over me. Though the winds blast up the hill, slamming at the house's gable, I feel warm, good.

Yesterday I stopped in Enniskillen to call on Mr. Boyle and Mrs. Cutler in the hospital. I had not been in Ireland for a year, but we have kept our correspondence up and I was anxious to see them.

Michael Boyle had been out of the hospital, had worked through the summer at the hay, but he had fallen ill again. His eyesight had failed and he could not recognize me until I spoke. He lay in bed, thin and drawn, moving little, while we talked of our mutual friends. His memory had failed, too; the happy thoughts he had put on tape had fled. I left his bedside and left the hospital, walking the cold town for hours alone.

The week before Christmas, Mrs. Cutler had suffered a heart attack. I went worried to her bed that night, but I was greatly relieved when I found her to be her bubbly, witty self. We chatted on about the health of our families and about the bombs that had rattled our windows the night before. Visiting hours brought a full court to her bedside and she performed for them with grand animation, twisting the language to her will.

Early this morning I walked out of the town and into a strong south wind, whistling reels, swinging my sack of stout from shoulder to shoulder without changing my stride. The low hills broke like a calm sea around me. North of Bellanaleck, two armored cars and an olive drab copter howled by. South of Bellanaleck, I met Tommy Love, bumping on his bicycle over the destruction which will become a new road to accomodate the monstrous lorries of the future.

"Is that yourself?," he said, "well, well, welcome home." Our friends made our conversation. He complimented Hugh Nolan for being able to manage so well without anyone to look after him. I gave him a photo I had taken of him a year before. "It's not so bad," he said, remounting his bike. He bumped away.

"All the best."

"Good bye."

"All the best now."

Mr. Love pedaled off to the store and I traveled the familiar pass across the springy bog, over the brae, and down to Hugh Nolan's. We downed a stout. He complimented his neighbors for generously looking after him. I made the tea while we talked politics. We could see no end to the troubles. Northern Ireland's shaky new government was already being attacked. It appeared that America's old government had been stolen by an irresponsible gang of neurotics. Mr. Nolan's cat population had grown, but there was no change in him. He was as bright and sharp as ever.

As winter's early dusk fell, I met Paddy McBrien on the lane. Two lean dogs scattered and dashed before him. He stood, lithe and hard, a rope over his shoulder to greet me. He had been tending his cattle, "sloughin and plowin after the cows." The hedges were dark, leafless, the fields a pale green. We talked of our talks in the past, of the time I had helped his sons and sons-in-law rook hay when he was ill. We agreed, sadly, that Michael Boyle and Joe Flanagan were in poor health. Mr. McBrien had been in the mumming squad with those men. His brother was Captain Mummer. He was Saint Patrick. He left me with a wish that we might meet in a pub before the Christmas season had ended, and I ascended the hill and turned over the field to the Flanagans. The underfoot pattern of soft and hard clay told me I was crossing old ridges. Oats had once grown there, though cows grazed it now.

While a little light remained to us, P and I went down to his garden where he had erected a great turf lump. We each filled a sack and shouldered it over the hill, bringing two days' supply of fuel into the kitchen.

Our dinner was superb: beef cooked to soft sweetness with carrots and onions in an oven hung over the fire. I complimented the dinner, mainly because it was excellent, and P used it as a case for his own theory of culture change. The old idea is good (beef tastes best cooked in an iron oven over an open turf fire). Outsiders, greedy for money, tell people their old ways are unfashionable, and the old idea is rejected (people buy ranges). The innovating generation soon recognizes they have made a mistake (beef is dry and tasteless when cooked on a range). However, they have committed themselves to the novelty, so they are forced to invent a rationalization for their acceptance of it (the beef is insipid, but the range is cleaner than the turf fire). The next generation, having never been exposed to the old idea, does not understand its virtues, and, therefore, does not realize that with progress comes degeneration (they have a clean range and don't know the beef tastes bad).

Like any worthwhile theory, P's model is broadly applicable. It works for mumming too. The old tradition is a bother (the turf fire is dirty; mumming required traveling in bad weather). But the old tradition has values that are not obvious (food tastes wonderful when cooked over a turf fire; mumming encouraged the sense of community). When the old ways die, the young do not know what they are missing (they go through life never quite satisfied with the food they eat; they go through life suspicious, lonely, and open to vague, harmful influences from without).

It was a night like most of ours together: there was no machine between us, no goal for our chat beyond friendship. We talked, drank up the stout, talked, took tea, talked, took tea, talked. Way past midnight, P prepared my bed. The wind howls at the tin roof. The little window over the hills of my bedding, beyond my feet, is black, ashy. P told me to huddle down in my bed. I have.

Toward the end of the night's conversation, P asked me a question. I was sitting on his creepie stool, leaning warmly against the backstone, against which, too, the fire was neatly heaped. Joe sat quietly at the corner opposite me, across the fire. P sat in the company seat in the middle. He didn't often have doctors of philosophy to query, so he asked, "Well, Henry, tell me this. How is it that education has advanced, but there are no great poets in the country like what there was in the past?"

I thought immediately of the fine local poets, Charlie Farmer, Hugh McGiveney, Mick Maguire. I had heard their songs from P, from Michael Boyle, from the great singer Oney McBrien who lives near Kinawley. Those men, who glittered in the generation before that of the men I know, were, truly, fine poets. Their senses of rhyme, rhythm, and humor were great. My thoughts spread out to the older musicians, falling back to the first time I had heard P touch the bow to his fiddle's strings, to the first time I had heard John Joe Maguire whose mellow fluting frightened me, it was so beautiful. And I thought of the music of the young people—flat, limp imitations of American country and western. "I don't know, P," I answered. "I really don't know."

I lie in the warm burrow I have dug in the bed, pondering just that. I don't know, but I need to know. I am a teacher. I am also a student, and I searched out Peter Flanagan, Hugh Nolan, Michael Boyle, and Ellen Cutler to teach me. To them I am an entertaining, occasional visitor. I may be of some use when I reinforce their traditions with my interest, but they don't need me. I need them. I need their memories, for without them an authentic history cannot be written, and I need history to understand how we have come to this pass and to consider alternatives for the future. I need their presence because they face the modern absurdity with good humor and great strength. I need their wisdom because they know and can explain a more sane social ethic than that of my own society. Without their teaching, I would find it hard to escape my culture and come closer to my self.

The wind breaks over the house. The window is black in the blackness. Wind and window. O, rare Peter hero. I don't know whether the wind kept up the whole night. I slept well.

1975

A black rainy night after a gray day in the year's first month, exactly a year since I have been in Ireland; I draw a chair up to the fire. My book on mumming is finished. A fat folder rests on my knees. Its contents are a year's correspondence from my teachers in Fermanagh.

They report the weather, the fortunes of the agricultural year, the progress of the new road. They speak often of the Troubles. Mrs. Cutler writes in the spring:

"Well dear, the times are still very bad in Belfast and Londonderry and all over. It is dreadful what people are killed in Belfast this last while. I don't know where it will end."

In the summer, Hugh Nolan writes:

"As far as both our countries are concerned the trouble is not over in either place. The strike here in the North caused a lot of inconvenience and trouble. The Explosion in Monaghan and Dublin caused many deaths + injuries but we hope with God's help that peace will come some day."

All the letters tell me of the health of friends and acquaintances. All contain wishes for our health and descriptions of that of their writers. Joe Flanagan was back in form shortly after I had seen him last, having made, as P writes, "a great recovery out of his sickness." Mrs. Cutler was released from the hospital in the middle of January. The summer found her feeling bad again, though still working to keep her flower garden looking nice: "My orange lilies are as high as myself." At Christmas she was back in the hospital and had undergone serious surgery, though from her last letter I learned that she was out of the hospital and that she had regained her strong and charming spirit. This winter, Hugh Nolan too had been in the hospital. A couple of days ago his letter of January eighth arrived in which he tells me that he was not seriously ill and, though the doctor had advised him to go into the hospital, he would not have gone except that his neighbors, who write his letters for him, "kept on the fires in the house," and helped him in general: "When it came to getting home, I wouldn't have got back to the house owing to having no one to look after me only that they took responsibility. Now I am back in form, thank God." Late last winter, I opened a letter from Hugh Nolan saying:

"You will be surprised to hear of Michael Boyle been dead. He died on 27th Jan. We were expecting him home. The change for the worse came suddenly. But I suppose it was God's Will that he was not to mend."

For the second time in my mature life, I wept openly. The first time was when I sat watching the news from Kent State.

The fire before me flares and snaps. The rain on the roof continues. The old ballad runs in my head: Fare thee well, Enniskillen, fare thee well for a while, with all your bright waters and every green isle, but when the war is over . . . .

The Irish Republican Army's delicate Christmastime truce seems to be failing. A log on the fire breaks, charred, flaming. The letters on my lap all close, as mine do, with a wish for future visits. "I hope I live to see you back in Ireland," Hugh Nolan writes. A letter from Mrs. Cutler says:

"I am just heart broke when you said in your letter yous

were not coming back to N. Ireland this year or what am I going to do, as I was looking forward to yous all coming up the lane or what on earth will I do."

P Flanagan writes:

"I sold 2 of my fiddles to the mothers of new beginners, but I am going to get another one and have it in real good tune when yous come back. Still we can see visions of Henry coming laughing across the hill."

I have visions, too, in the bright fire.

Glossary

IRISH ENGLISH carries constant evidence of translation from Irish Gaelic, even when it comes off the lips of people who have never spoken Irish. Syntax is surprising, words derived from Irish are sprinkled through any statement, and, more confusingly, English words are used in very special ways. What follows is not an attempt at a complete glossary, but a list of words from this book which seemed to deserve further comment. All of the glosses are designed to represent only the speech of this part of south Fermanagh. G. B. Adams, ed., *Ulster Dialects: An Introductory Symposium* (Belfast: Ulster Folk Museum, 1964), provides good general background and bibliography. Rev. Patrick S. Dinneen's *An Irish-English Dictionary* (Dublin: Educational Company of Ireland for the Irish Texts Society, 1970, first published 1927) is very helpful. Michael Traynor, *The English Dialect of Donegal: A Glossary* (Dublin: The Royal Irish Academy, 1953), gives meanings which are regularly close to those of Ballymenone.

BEAST   Any animal might be classed a beast, but a cow is generally meant.

BESOM   A broom, homemade of bog heather.

BOY   Immature males are not called boys; they are "cubs," "youngsters," and sometimes "lads." "Boys" are unmarried adult men and men, married or not, who are out in all male company, working or playing. (Compare the American: "the boys down at the office," "he's a good old boy.")

BRAE   Used interchangeably with "hill."

Besom and creepie at the Flanagans' hearth

CEILI   This is usually spelled *ceilidh* and it usually implies a party with musical entertainment. I adopted the spelling of Ulster folklorists, Michael J. Murphy (*Tyrone Folk Quest*) and Sam Hanna Bell (*Erin's Orange Lily*), so the word could appear freshly and draw in its full meaning. "To ceili" means about what "to visit" means in the southern United States: the ceili is an informal, usually small, evening gathering of friends in a house for conversation, probably tea, possibly music. The word is bent to many grammatical intents: At twilight, a ceilier goes off on his ceili to a ceili in a ceiliing house where he will ceili on till daylight.

CHAPEL   Catholic country churches are always called "chapels," Protestant ones, "churches." This reflects on the history of oppression and the present state of tense courtesy: the words Catholic and Protestant are avoided; people generally speak of "our side," "the other side."

CONACRE   Traditional land rentals work differently in different parts of Ireland. Here the land is "let" for eleven months at a time, so that the person who "takes" the land has rights to the land's seasonal produce (in Irish, *conác* means property, wealth) but not to the land itself. He may, for example, cut a year's turf out of "conacre bog." Such arrangements are usually made between farmers and widows or men who do not farm. The renter may use the land fully, but only in the way the land's owner would use it; he may not, for example, build a house on conacre bog because during one month of the year, generally December, the bog will revert to its owner's possession.

CORN   Though this word can refer to wheat or rye as well, it usually means oats. Oats, once grown for grain for bread, are now grown for thatching material, so they are still often "sheared" close to the ground with a "shearin hook" in order to obtain the longest possible straw. Some consider the use of a scythe in a field of oats a degenerate modern practice. The cut oats are bundled into sheaves which are built into "stooks" to dry before they are "lashed" or "slashed" for use in roofing. The concept of corn has great power; the good person has "the heart of corn."

COT   A square ended, plank-built boat, descended from the dug-out canoe, which was most recently used for agricultural transport between the islands of Lough Erne. Many of Ireland's lakes have their distinctive cot forms; Erne is no exception. See: Francis Fitzpatrick, "A Lough Erne Cot," *Clogher Record*, I:3 (1955), pp. 118–120; Michael McCaughan, "The Lough Erne Cot," *Ulster Folk Museum Year Book* (1969/70), pp. 5–8.

CREEPIE   A low wooden stool, set by the hearth and used to get close to the fire. Small and light, it creeps over the floor with you while you sit on it. (See the illustrations on pp. 46 and 154.)

CROOKS   This is the collective term for the iron chains and trammels from which pots, kettles, ovens, and pans hang over the fire. The crooks, in turn, may hang from a pole high in the chimney or from a socketed, pivoting "crane crook." (See the illustration on p. 46.)

DELPH   Delph is the crockery—not necessarily delftware—displayed on the open shelves of the upper half of the kitchen's

Fadge in the oven at Mrs. Cutler's hearth

dresser. There is usually one shelf for cups, one for plates, and one for platters, mostly English willowware or pottery from the old and famous Fermanagh pottery at Belleek. This spelling, used by Michael J. Murphy (*Tyrone Folk Quest*) and James Joyce (*Finnegans Wake*: 304), gets the local pronunciation right. (For dressers, see the illustrations on pp. 6, 15, 30, and 47.)

FADGE In eastern Ulster, "fadge" is potato bread. Here potato bread is "prettie bread" ("pretties" being synonymous with "potatoes" or "spuds") and "fadge" is the soda bread baked in an iron oven in the range or on the hearth. Fadge comes as a round "cake." Using similar recipes, some women make a low, yellow, and crumbly fadge, others make it high, white, and smooth. Either way it is excellent.

FAIRY The fairies are the angels cast out of Heaven with Lucifer. They stand to the height of a six-year-old child and embody the irrational in existence, replacing healthy babies with strange changelings, enticing people into forgetting responsibilities, oddly offering and denying wealth. They live in the "forths" at the hill-tops and can be heard making the world's most beguiling music as they travel the passes between the forths. They are to be feared, respected, avoided.

FRIEND In this book I have not used the traditional meaning for "friend": a (sometimes rather distant) blood relative.

HEDGE Generally planted up on a "ditch" (a sod wall along which a drain runs), hedges are made of trimmed thorn bushes and include numerous trees. Hedges, thus, not only divide fields and control stock, they are the source of wood: whatever is made of wood is "cut out of the hedge."

HALF-ONE The standard bar measure of whiskey or wine, "a half glass," a quarter of a gill.

JOIN A formal association established for some collective end: sharing draft animals, tools, labor, or food and drink at a party held in a home. The group ethic runs so deep that, as a verb, join means not only to gather people, tools, effort, or money, but even "to begin"—"he joined to work in the bog on his lone"—the un-spoken assumption in the language being that you cannot begin an endeavor alone.

JORUM A small quantity of drink.

LAD A commonly used, all purpose noun, comparable to "thing" or "stuff" in America. Michael Boyle called Prince George's breast-plate "a lad"; Mrs. Cutler called the relish we introduced into our dinners with her, "that green lad."

LOCK A small amount of hay is "a lock of hay," analogous to a lock of hair. Possibly from that usage, the word expanded to mean a small quantity of anything built up of similar units—"a lock of turf," "a lock of days," "a lock of coppers."

MEARN A boundary between properties or townlands, usually marked by a drain. As a verb, "to mearn" means "to adjoin." (In Irish, *mear* is an act of judgment, a measure.)

METHAL   This Irish word is variously spelled—meiteal, meitheal, metheil, mechal—though "methal" seems to represent the Ballymenone pronunciation best. Generally a methal is an emergency assemblage of workers, though any work group can be called a methal: "A methal of men joined to win the hay."

OIL   The "paraffin oil" (kerosene in American English) burned in lamps and kept in tins by the hearth to light the fire.

OLD-FASHIONED   This is a spatial rather than a temporal concept. The "old-fashioned" person is shy, backward, withdrawn. Thus the irony that the more modern and individualistic people are (the more they watch TV rather than ceili), the more they are—in local terms—"old-fashioned."

PASS   A generally unmarked right-of-way over the fields or bogs. There are "passes"—or "pads"—for fairies as well as for human beings.

POTEEN   Also called "moonshine" and "mountain dew," this is the locally made whiskey which was once commonly distilled from oats on Lough Erne's islands. It is still concocted in the hills along the border, though now it is made from sugar with no grain base and has fallen from popularity.

PUIR   This is an attempt to capture a subtly special pronunciation of the word "poor." Such pronunciation is consciously Irish and is called "speaking broad." When poor and old are pronounced puir and ould a sense of warm familiarity is added to the normal connotations those words carry: a "puir" person is poor and deserving of affection; something that is "ould" is old and ours.

RAMAS   Poetry pleasantly belittled. The poems written in adolescence, for instance, are old ramases. In Irish, *ramán* is a burst of song.

ROOK   Once cut hay has dried sufficiently in rows, it is raked into "rings" and built into conical "rooks." Later the rooks are hauled to the "haggard," the yard behind the dwelling, where the hay is piled under sheds or built into large, thatched circular stacks called "pecks." G. B. Adams has written an excellent paper, "The Work and Words of Haymaking," *Ulster Folklife*, 12(1966), pp. 66–91; 13(1967), pp. 29–53; he uses the spelling "ruck."

SALLY ROD   "Sally rods," "sallies" or "willies" are the branches of the willows cultivated in "sally gardens" for a variety of purposes —weaving baskets, making scollops for thatch, and rings for mummers' hats.

SLAP BRICK   Named from the action of slapping clay into molds, slap bricks were made along the Arney River in the nineteenth and early twentieth centuries. The blue clay was dug, mixed ("soughed") in pits, molded into bricks that were spread out to dry, turned up on edge in rows, then built into successively larger "hacks" and "stacks" before being built ("crowded") into corbeled kilns. Many of the local houses were constructed of this handmade brick.

SPADE   The Irish spade, of which the Fermanagh variant is an extreme example, is a cultivating tool, a sort of hand plow. It is used to mark out ("nick") and turn over ("cope") the ground to create the "ridges" in which vegetables are planted. The "turf spade"—called a slane in the literature—is a different implement, used to punch the wet turf into brick-shaped sections for drying into fuel. Together the two spades are the basic tools of the local farmer who still works the soil; he calls them his "weapons." Much has been written on Irish spades and their use; see the papers by Evans, Gailey, Ó Danachair, Lucas, and O'Sullivan in Alan Gailey and Alexander Fenton, eds., *The Spade in Northern and Atlantic Europe* (Belfast: Ulster Folk Museum and Institute of Irish Studies, Queen's University, 1970).

STREET   The paved—cobbled or cemented—area directly in front of the home's front door. Thus, a muddy lane may become a paved street for a short section in front of the house; a house removed from a lane will often have its piece of street on which you leave

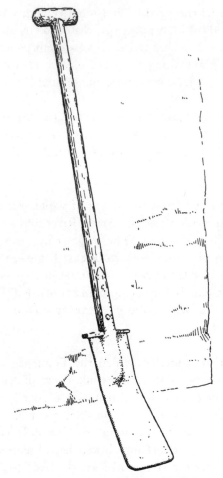

The south Fermanagh spade

the worst of the mud off your boots before passing through the front door. An American would best think of a "street" as the floor of a missing front porch.

STROOP   The teapot's spout.

TEA   While tea obviously means tea, and usually richly creamed and sugared tea, "to take tea" implies that some food, usually bread and butter, perhaps bread and jam and "biscuits" (cookies) will accompany the hot liquid.

Glossary

TERRIBLE An exaggerative adjective with positive connotations, comparable to the "wonderful" or "terrific" of American speech.

TURF Peat is always called turf. It is taken from the Irish bogs in several ways. Here, it is all cut underfoot with a "turf spade," loaded into "turf barrows" and "wheeled" to be "spread" where it lies until it is dry enough to be built into "clamps." For permanent storage, it is built into "lumps" in the bog or "stacks" near the house or piled up in a "turf house."

WELLINGTON Black, knee-high rubber boots, much like the boots of early nineteenth century military officers. Wellingtons are the usual footwear in this very wet climate.

WIN To win means to conquer wet nature in dry, manmade forms—turf clamps, hay rooks. Nature's substances are won when they have been altered for human benefit.

Library of African Literature. Oxford: Oxford University Press, 1967.

JACOBS, MELVILLE, *The Content and Style of an Oral Literature*: *Clackamas Chinook Myths and Tales*. Chicago: University of Chicago Press, 1959.

LÉVI-STRAUSS, CLAUDE (John and Doreen Weightman, trans.), *The Raw and the Cooked: Introduction to a Science of Mythology*, I. New York: Harper and Row, 1970.

LORD, ALBERT B., *The Singer of Tales*. New York: Atheneum, 1965.

MERRIAM, ALAN P., *Ethnomusicology of the Flathead Indians*, Viking Fund Publications in Anthropology, 44. Chicago: Aldine, 1967.

PEACOCK, JAMES L., *Rites of Modernization: Symbolic and Social Aspects of Indonesian Proletarian Drama*. Chicago: University of Chicago Press, 1968.

TURNER, VICTOR, *The Forest of Symbols*: *Aspects of Ndembu Ritual*. Ithaca: Cornell University Press, 1967.

All of the works listed above, whether by folklorists or not, are examples of the kind of study performed—or wished for—by many modern folklorists. If you would like some feeling for the past and contemporary norms of folklore scholarship, the *Journal of American Folklore, Journal of the Folklore Institute, Folklore, Folk Life*, and the books listed below will provide some introduction. These books are all frequently used as texts in folklore classes; that edited by Richard Dorson includes a good survey on "Folk Drama" by Roger Abrahams.

BRUNVAND, JAN HAROLD, *The Study of American Folklore: An Introduction*. New York: W. W. Norton, 1968.

DORSON, RICHARD M., ed., *Folklore and Folklife: An Introduction*. Chicago: University of Chicago Press, 1972.

DUNDES, ALAN, ed., *The Study of Folklore*. Englewood Cliffs: Prentice-Hall, 1965.

During the half year before I left for Ireland in June, 1972, I wrote two overtly theoretical works. Although there were changes

Bibliography

in my thought between the article and the book and more between them and this book, they discuss many of the ideas that guided me during my fieldwork and they bring to the surface many of the essentially structuralist theories embedded in this bit of mummery.

Folk Housing in Middle Virginia: A Structural Analysis of the Historical Artifact. Knoxville: University of Tennessee Press, 1975.
  "Structure and Function, Folklore and the Artifact," *Semiotica,* vii:4 (1973), pp. 313-351.

MUMMING

Much has been written on mumming. Most of it concerns various survivalistic propositions and the possible relations between mumming and the history of Western drama. Even authors who take such goals as primary do provide texts of the plays, if little in the way of description of performance. Alan Gailey's work is exceptional in giving excellent information on regional variation. The book by Cawte, Helm, and Peacock is a useful tool and could form the foundation for a sophisticated endeavor in cultural geography. A full break in the tradition of mumming scholarship is marked by the volume edited by Halpert and Story; it concentrates on recent, knowable history and presents superb anthropologically ordered description and analysis. In addition to journal articles and the fine small books issued by the Guizer Press, these are the main mumming works:

BRODY, ALAN, *The English Mummers and Their Plays: Traces of Ancient Mystery*, Publications in Folklore and Folklife. Philadelphia: University of Pennsylvania Press, 1970.
  CAWTE, E. C., ALEX HELM, and N. PEACOCK, *English Ritual Drama: A Geographical Index.* London: The Folk-Lore Society, 1967.
  CHAMBERS, E. K., *The English Folk-Play,* New York: Russell and Russell, 1964, reprint of 1933 edition.
  GAILEY, ALAN, *Irish Folk Drama.* Cork: Mercier Press, 1969.
  HALPERT, HERBERT, and G. M. STORY, eds., *Christmas Mum-*

ming in Newfoundland: Essays in Anthropology, Folklore, and History. Toronto: University of Toronto Press for Memorial University of Newfoundland, 1969.

TIDDY, R. J. E., *The Mummers' Play*. Oxford: Oxford University Press, 1923.

IRELAND

Located at Europe's Atlantic margin, artistically rich, Ireland invites study. In general, most anthropological research and most studies of oral narrative have been oriented toward the Irish-speaking West. This emphasis has been balanced, owing to the bright particular genius of E. Estyn Evans, by geographical research and studies of artifacts in the North. The south Ulster hills, in which Fermanagh lies, have been less attractive to scholars, though the reader can get a feeling for the area and its traditions from the writings of T. G. F. Paterson and Michael J. Murphy from Armagh, and Patrick Kavanagh from Monaghan. In his book on John Maguire, Robin Morton provides information that is closely comparable to that in this book, for Maguire lives only a few miles south of Ballymenone. Irish traditional culture is exquisitely represented in a strong number of autobiographies, biographies, and portraits of individual makers of the culture. Some of the best are:

CROSS, ERIC, *The Tailor and Ansty*. New York: Devin-Adair, 1964, first published 1942.

DOYLE, LYNN, *An Ulster Childhood*. London: Duckworth, 1927, first published 1921.

KAVANAGH, PATRICK, *The Green Fool*. London: Martin Brian and O'Keeffe, 1971, first published 1938.

LITTLE, GEORGE A., *Malachi Horan Remembers*. Dublin: M. H. Gill, 1943.

MORTON, ROBIN, *Come Day, Go Day, God Send Sunday: The Songs and Life Story, Told in His Own Words, of John Maguire, Traditional Singer and Farmer from Co. Fermanagh*. London: Routledge and Kegan Paul, 1973.

Ó CROHAN, TOMAŚ (Robin Flower, trans.), *The Islandman*. Oxford: Oxford University Press, 1951.

Bibliography

O'DONOGHUE, JOHN, *In a Quiet Land*. London: The Country Book Club, 1959.

O'SULLIVAN, MAURICE (Moya Llewelyn Davies and George Thomson, trans.), *Twenty Years A-Growing*. New York: The Viking Press, 1933.

SAYERS, PEIG (Seamus Ennis, trans.), *An Old Woman's Reflections*. London: Oxford University Press, 1962.

Several excellent descriptions of Irish areas or communities have been published. These differ because Ireland does and also because such studies operate like projective tests for ethnographers. The depiction of an individual, say Eric Cross's Tailor, is limited by the subject's reality, but a community is complex and composed of people of every temper, and a scholar's training and personality will cause him to create the community in a way no other scholar would—in a way that reinforces the importance of his own interests, the correctness of his own attitudes. Any ethnography is rhetorical as well as empirical, fictional as well as true, so people who wish to understand an area's culture should read as much as possible, or they should read nothing at all and go there. Some interesting descriptions:

ARENSBERG, CONRAD, *The Irish Countryman*: *An Anthropological Study*. Garden City: Natural History Press, 1968, first published 1937.

ARENSBERG, CONRAD M., and SOLON T. KIMBALL, *Family and Community in Ireland*. Cambridge: Harvard University Press, 1968, first published 1940.

BRODY, HUGH, *Inishkillane*: *Change and Decline in the West of Ireland*. New York: Schocken Books, 1974.

EVANS, E. ESTYN, *Mourne Country*: *Landscape and Life in South Down*. Dundalk: W. Tempest, Dundalgan Press, 1967, first published 1951.

FLOWER, ROBIN, *The Western Island*: *or, the Great Blasket*. New York: Oxford University Press, 1945.

MESSENGER, JOHN C., *Inis Beag*: *Isle of Ireland*, Case Studies in Cultural Anthropology. New York: Holt, Rinehart and Winston, 1969.

MURPHY, MICHAEL J., *At Slieve Gullion's Foot*. Dundalk: W. Tempest, Dundalgan Press, 1945.

MURPHY, MICHAEL J., *Tyrone Folk Quest*. Belfast: Blackstaff Press, 1973.

SYNGE, JOHN M., *The Aran Islands*. Dublin: Maunsel and Company, 1906.

Each of the two Irelands has its great reservoir of folkloristic energies. The island has two fine journals, *Ulster Folklife* and *Béaloideas*, and two main groups of scholars. In the North there is the circle around E. Estyn Evans: R. H. Buchanan, Alan Gailey, Desmond McCourt, George Thompson. In Dublin, A. T. Lucas, Caoimhín Ó Danachair (Kevin Danaher), Séamus Ó Duilearga (J. H. Delargy), and Seán Ó Súilleabháin (Sean O'Sullivan) have led in the study of Irish folk culture. Together these men have produced a statement both broad and deep on the nature of the Irish land, its people, their labor and art. Some of the best summaries of Irish traditions or the Irish tradition follow:

BELL, SAM HANNA, *Erin's Orange Lily*. London: Dennis Dobson, 1956.

BREATHNACH, BREANDÁN, *Folkmusic and Dances of Ireland*. Dublin: Talbot Press, 1971.

BUCHANAN, RONALD H., "Calendar Customs," *Ulster Folklife*, 8 (1962), pp. 15–34; 9 (1963), pp. 61–79.

DANAHER, KEVIN, *Gentle Places and Simple Things*. Cork: Mercier Press, 1964.

DANAHER, KEVIN, *In Ireland Long Ago*. Cork: Mercier Press, 1962.

DANAHER, KEVIN, *Irish Country People*. Cork: Mercier Press, 1966.

DANAHER, KEVIN, *The Pleasant Land of Ireland*. Cork: Mercier Press, 1970.

DANAHER, KEVIN, *The Year in Ireland*. Cork: Mercier Press, 1972.

DELARGY, J. H., "The Gaelic Story-Teller. With Some Notes on Gaelic Folk-Tales," *Proceedings of the British Academy* (1945), pp. 177–221.

Bibliography

EVANS, E. ESTYN, *Irish Folk Ways*. New York: Devin-Adair, 1957.

EVANS, E. ESTYN, *Irish Heritage: The Landscape, The People and Their Work*. Dundalk: W. Tempest, Dundalgan Press, 1963, first published 1942.

EVANS, E. ESTYN, *The Personality of Ireland: Habitat, Heritage, and History*. Cambridge: Cambridge University Press, 1973.

MACNEILL, MÁIRE, *The Festival of Lughnasa: A Study of the Survival of the Celtic Festival of the Beginning of Harvest*. London: Oxford University Press, 1962.

MERCIER, VIVIAN, *The Irish Comic Tradition*. New York: Oxford University Press, 1969.

Ó SÚILLEABHAIN, SEÁN, *A Handbook of Irish Folklore*. Hatboro: Folklore Associates, 1963, reprint of 1942 edition.

Ó SÚILLEABHAIN, SEÁN, *Irish Folk Custom and Belief*, Irish Life and Culture, XV. Dublin: Cultural Relations Committee, n.d., c. 1970.

Ó SÚILLEABHAIN, SEÁN, *Irish Wake Amusements*. Cork: Mercier Press, 1967.

O'SULLIVAN, SEAN, *Folktales of Ireland*, Folktales of the World. Chicago: University of Chicago Press, 1966.

ZIMMERMANN, GEORGES-DENIS, *Songs of Irish Rebellion: Political Street Ballads and Rebel Songs: 1780–1900*. Hatboro: Folklore Associates, 1967.

Notes

SURVIVAL

1. The quotation is from the first page of the preface, "This Book," in W. B. Yeats, *The Celtic Twilight* (New York: New American Library, 1962, first published 1893), p. 31. Yeats has left us a great bounty of autobiographical writing. Six of these documents have been gathered as *The Autobiography of William Butler Yeats* (New York: Collier, 1974), which provides fine material for understanding Yeats and his times. For my argument, particularly valuable commentary can be found on pp. 21, 51, 76–79, 93–102, 127–132, 145–146, 159, 178–184, 193–196, 247–254, 263–272, 318, 338.

2. His continuing relevance has created an enormous scholarship on Morris. J. W. Mackail's *The Life of William Morris* is once more available (New York: Benjamin Blom, 1968, first published 1899). A good recent study is Paul Thompson, *The Work of William Morris* (New York: Viking, 1967). A handy sampler of his thought is Asa Briggs, ed., *William Morris: Selected Writings and Designs* (Baltimore: Penguin Books, 1962). During the period when Yeats was having Sunday suppers with the artists, socialists, and anarchists at Morris' home, Morris was working on two prose romances which are excellent introductions to his thought: *A Dream of John Ball* (first published in book form in 1889) and *News from Nowhere* (first published as a book in 1891).

3. "The Second Coming" was published in 1920. Yeats quoted part of it in a little essay on the medieval Unity of Being which is section 22 of his autobiography, *The Trembling of the Veil* (*The Autobiography*, p. 130). The poem's full text can be found in Peter Allt and Russell K. Alspach, eds., *The Variorum Edition of the Poems of W. B. Yeats* (New York: Macmillan, 1965), pp. 401–402.

4. This paragraph's information on Joyce is all from Stanislaus Joyce (Richard Ellmann, ed), *My Brother's Keeper: James Joyce's Early Years* (New York: Viking, 1958), pp. 98–99, 144–145, 195, and especially 220–224. Yeats' evaluation of the book can be found in W. B. Yeats, *Essays and Introductions* (New York: Collier, 1972), p. 211. Yeats' opinion is accurately reported in James Joyce's *Ulysses* (New York: Random House, 1934, first published 1922), p. 213. The closing quotation is from Lady Gregory, *Visions and Beliefs in the West of Ireland* (New York: Oxford University Press, 1970, reprint of 1920 edition), p. 15.

5. E. K. Chambers, *The English Folk-Play* (New York: Russell and Russell, 1964, reprint of 1933 edition), p. 12.

6. I have taken Yeats' attitudes on folklore primarily from *The Autobiography*, p. 386; *Essays and Introductions*, p. 516; Yeats' notes to Lady Gregory's *Visions and Beliefs*; and William Butler Yeats, *Fairy and Folk Tales of the Irish Peasantry*, the 1888 work reprinted in *Fairy and Folk Tales of Ireland* (New York: Macmillan, 1973), pp. 6–7.

7. A recent paper on "The Origin of the Mummers' Play" by E. T. Kirby, *Journal of American Folklore*, 84:333 (July–September 1971), pp. 275–288, opens with an attack on the usual Frazerian interpretation, only to replace it with another survivalistic explanation. His revisionist position led to a controversy in the *Journal of American Folklore*, 85:338 (October–December 1972), pp. 375–376; 86:341 (July–September 1973) pp. 282–285; 87:345 (July–September 1974), pp. 250–252.

8. For the critique of the myth-ritual notion, see: William Bascom, "The Myth-Ritual Theory," *Journal of American Folklore*, 70:276 (April–June 1957), pp. 103–114; Joseph Fontenrose, *The Ritual Theory of Myth*, Folklore Studies, 18 (Berkeley and Los Angeles: University of California Press, 1971). The personalities who argued around the beginnings of the idea of survivalism are well described in Richard M. Dorson, *The British Folklorists: A History* (Chicago: University of Chicago Press, 1968), chapters v–viii.

9. Alan Gailey, *Irish Folk Drama* (Cork: Mercier Press, 1969), pp. 8–9.

10. A characteristic comment by Sir James Frazer comes in *The Golden Bough: A Study in Magic and Religion*, 12 vols. (Lon-

don: Macmillan, 1955, reprint of the third edition of 1907–1915), on p. 214 of the fourth volume where he says that folk custom tends "with the growth of civilisation, to dwindle from solemn ritual into mere pageant and pastime. . . ." Vivian Mercier concludes his excellent book, *The Irish Comic Tradition* (New York: Oxford University Press, 1969) with a witty critique of the scholastic inability to see the humor in myth and ritual.

11. Alan Brody, *The English Mummers and Their Plays: Traces of Ancient Mystery*, Publications in Folklore and Folklife (Philadelphia: University of Pennsylvania Press, 1970), fn. p. 17.

12. Tristram P. Coffin advances the idea of a ballad's progress from narrative to lyric in "The Traditional Ballad as an Art Form," in *The British Traditional Ballad in North America*, Bibliographic and Special Series, II (Philadelphia: American Folklore Society, 1963), pp. 164–172.

13. Roger D. Abrahams presents West Indian texts and a careful discussion relating them to printed and oral texts from Britain in " 'Pull Out Your Purse and Pay': A St. George Mumming from the British West Indies," *Folklore,* 79 (Autumn 1968), pp. 176–201.

14. The effects of framing in art are described in Rudolf Arnheim, *Art and Visual Perception: A Psychology of the Creative Eye* (Berkeley and Los Angeles: University of California Press, 1971), pp. 9–11, 231–233; and in the second chapter of Christian Metz (Michael Taylor, trans.), *Film Language: A Semiotics of the Cinema* (New York: Oxford University Press, 1974).

15. Yeats' early essays in question are those of *Ideas of Good and Evil*, reprinted as the first section of *Essays and Introductions*. All have bearing on the Romantic Argument, though the first, tenth and eleventh are the most important and the last part of "The Symbolism of Poetry," pp. 163–164, provides his most intense statement. One of these early papers, "The Happiest of Poets," is on Morris (pp. 53–64). John Ruskin was greatly influential. The mature James Frazer and the teenaged James Joyce both imitated his style; Ruskin is one of the writers parodied in *Ulysses*. Two of Ruskin's early works provided Victorian romantic thought with great impetus and direction: *The Seven Lamps of Architecture* (1849, revised 1855, 1880), and *The Stones of Venice* (1851–1853). His essay "The Nature of Gothic," in the second volume of *The*

Stones of Venice (London: Smith, Elder, 1853) was a principal seminal statement of nineteenth century romanticism.

16. Two important instances of modern thinking in anthropology are Alan P. Merriam, *The Anthropology of Music* (Evanston: Northwestern University Press, 1964), and Robert Plant Armstrong, *The Affecting Presence: An Essay in Humanistic Anthropology* (Urbana: University of Illinois Press, 1971). Merriam's interest in synesthesia and reluctance to allow a separate aesthetic category in non-Western art, and Armstrong's discovery of similar properties in different cultural expressions both exemplify our attempt to escape easy, rationalistic conceptualizing. Probably the two most influential modernist works in linguistics have been Ferdinand de Saussure (Wade Baskin, trans.), *Course in General Linguistics* (New York: McGraw-Hill, 1966, first published 1915), and Noam Chomsky, *Syntactic Structures*, Janua Linguarum, 4 (The Hague: Mouton, 1957). With regard to the matter at hand, particularly valuable statements by Claude Lévi-Strauss can be found in chapters two, four, and nine of (Claire Jacobson and Brooke Grundfest Schoepf, trans.) *Structural Anthropology* (New York: Doubleday, 1967); *The Savage Mind* (Chicago: University of Chicago Press, 1966); and the Overture to (John and Doreen Weightman, trans.) *The Raw and the Cooked: Introduction to a Science of Mythology*, I (New York: Harper and Row, 1970).

17. The structuralist goal is lucidly set forth in Jean Piaget (Chaninah Maschler, trans.), *Structuralism* (New York: Basic Books, 1970).

18. Claude Lévi-Strauss' feelings on modern painting and musical supremacy are expressed in the Overture to *The Raw and the Cooked* and in the later two-thirds of G. Charbonnier (John and Doreen Weightman, trans.), *Conversations with Claude Lévi-Strauss* (London: Jonathan Cape, 1969). Joyce's friend, the painter Frank Budgen, often compares Joyce's work with painting and says that Joyce had a feeling for the visual arts, though he makes it clear that Joyce's interest in painting was slight in contrast with his love for music: *James Joyce and the Making of Ulysses* (Bloomington: Indiana University Press, 1960, first published 1934), pp. 37, 133–138, 154, 173–174, 181–186, 244, 325–326, 328. Lévi-Strauss says myth and his analysis of it are like music;

Joyce says *Finnegans Wake* is not like music: it is music. The influence of music upon his art is stressed by Kandinsky in his "Reminiscences," in Robert L. Herbert, ed., *Modern Artists on Art* (Englewood Cliffs: Prentice-Hall, 1964), pp. 19–44, especially 26–27, 30–33. Paul Klee and his wife were musicians. His early diaries were made of comments on the concerts he played and heard, the paintings he created and saw. The later diaries describe his trip to Tunisia and his life during World War I which he endured like Joyce, thinking about art. See: Felix Klee, ed. *The Diaries of Paul Klee: 1898–1918* (Berkeley and Los Angeles: University of California Press, 1968), particularly pp. 177, 228–245, 290, 310–312. Both of the painters wrote several important works. Their protostructural concepts were revealingly set out in Wassily Kandinsky (Michael Sadleir, trans.), *Concerning the Spiritual in Art*, The Documents of Modern Art, 5 (New York: George Wittenborn, 1964, first published 1912), and Paul Klee (Paul Findlay, trans.), *On Modern Art* (London: Faber and Faber, 1969, first presented 1924).

19. Yeats' opinions come from "A General Introduction for My Work," in *Essays and Introductions*, particularly pp. 516, 522. The most remarkable statement of these thoughts exists in an account Yeats wrote, but did not publish, of an encounter in 1902 between himself and the youthful Joyce. To Joyce's criticism of his reliance on folklore Yeats countered that all great work, including Joyce's, comes ultimately "from the folk"; art removed from the folk spirit becomes individualistic and degenerate. Richard Ellmann discusses this document in several of his excellent works and gives it in full in *The Identity of Yeats* (New York: Oxford University Press, 1968, first published 1954), pp. 85–89.

20. Wright's important essays here are "The Art and Craft of the Machine" and "The Sovereignty of the Individual." The quotation is from the latter, p. 85 in Edgar Kaufman and Ben Raeburn, eds., *Frank Lloyd Wright: Writings and Buildings* (Cleveland and New York: World, 1969).

21. See Wassily Kandinsky and Franz Marc (Henning Falkenstein, trans.), *The Blaue Reiter Almanac*, Documents of 20th-Century Art (New York: Viking, 1974, first published 1912), especially Kandinsky's contribution, "On the Question of Form," pp. 147–187.

22. Antonin Artaud (Mary Caroline Richards, trans.), *The Theater and Its Double* (New York: Grove Press, 1958, first published 1938).

23. Bertolt Brecht (John Willett, trans.), "A Short Organum for the Theatre," in Toby Cole, ed., *Playwrights on Playwriting: The Meaning and Making of Modern Drama from Ibsen to Ionesco* (New York: Hill and Wang, 1960, essay from 1948), pp. 72–105.

24. See "Certain Noble Plays of Japan" in Yeats' *Essays and Introductions*. His comments in the papers "At Stratford-on-Avon," and "Discoveries" in the same volume, as well as the attitude toward Ibsen dropped in *The Autobiography*, p. 185, are also revealing. Yeats' most enjoyable annoyance at Ibsen is to be found in the comical introduction to *A Vision* (New York: Collier, 1972, first published 1926). The characters there take their names from the famous Irish version of Aarne-Thompson *The Types of the Folktale*, F.F.C., 184 (Helsinki: Suomalainen Tiedeakatemia, 1961), number 1535, "Huddon, Duddon, and Donald O'Leary," which Hugh Nolan told me masterfully one afternoon while we waited for the group to gather for a visit to Michael Boyle in the hospital. Yeats put the tale "Donald and His Neighbors" in *Fairy and Folk Tales of the Irish Peasantry*. In *A Vision* (pp. 33–35), Daniel O'Leary flings his boots at the actors in a fashionable realistic drama.

25. Sean O'Casey, *Inishfallen Fare Thee Well* (New York: Macmillan, 1960), pp. 372–376.

26. Samuel Beckett's warning comes in the opening pages of his initial essay in *Our Exagmination Round His Factification for Incamination of Work in Progress* (New York: New Directions, 1972, first published 1929).

Geography

1. A. J. B. Wace, "North Greek Festivals and the Worship of Dionysos," *The Annual of the British School at Athens*, XVI (1909–1910), pp. 233–237. That article, running pp. 232–253, and another by the same author in the same journal, "Mumming Plays in the Southern Balkans," XIX (1912–1913), pp. 248–265, include

other descriptions of similar plays. A modern scholar provides the larger setting of such plays in George A. Megas, *Greek Calendar Customs* (Athens: B. and M. Rhodis, 1963), pp. 37–52, 60–67.

2. A great many English play texts are available. A goodly bunch were brought together in R. J. E. Tiddy's *The Mummers' Play* (Oxford: Oxford University Press, 1923), pp. 144–257. E. C. Cawte, Alex Helm, and N. Peacock in *English Ritual Drama*: *A Geographical Index* (London: The Folk-Lore Society, 1967) provide an excellent index and bibliography for British mumming as well as a few sample texts. The generalizations about mumming in Wexford and eastern Ulster come from Alan Gailey's *Irish Folk Drama*, pp. 17–35, 49. For a couple of especially good reports from eastern Ulster: Alan Gailey, "The Rhymers of South-East Antrim," *Ulster Folklife*, 13 (1967), pp. 18–28; Michael McCaughan, "Christmas Rhymers in the Donaghadee Area," *Ulster Folklife*, 14 (1968), pp. 66–70. The southwestern Ulster traits are isolated in E. R. R. Green, "Christmas Rhymers and Mummers," *Ulster Journal of Archaeology*, 3rd Series, 9 (1946), pp. 10, 12; Alan Gailey, *Christmas Rhymers and Mummers in Ireland* (Ibstock, Leicestershire: Guizer Press, 1968), pp. 17, 35.

3. Sean O'Sullivan provides a short history of the Irish Folklore Commission in the Introduction to his fine *Folktales of Ireland*, Folktales of the World (Chicago: University of Chicago Press, 1966). A good description of the Ulster Folk Museum's development can be found in George Thompson, "The Ulster Folk Museum," in Michael Longley, ed., *Causeway*: *The Arts in Ulster* (Belfast: Arts Council of Northern Ireland, 1971), pp. 153–170.

4. Cawte, Helm, and Peacock, *English Ritual Drama*, p. 70, list sixteen Fermanagh texts. One of those—that for Bellanaleck—is that of the Ballymenone mummers. In my hunts in the archives, I found that it was recorded by Alexander McConnell from Andrew Boyle in 1947 and is in Dublin, U.D.C. Belfield in IFC vol. 1090, pp. 111–118, and from Michael Boyle in 1954 and is in the files of the Ulster Folk Museum, Holywood, County Down, in McConnell's notebook, pp. 39–45.

5. Fermanagh Mummings: Lisnaskea: Michael J. Murphy, collector, IFC vol. 1696, pp. 227, 232–233, 259–260. Knockninny: Michael J. Murphy, collector, IFC vol. 1696, pp. 179–180, 214–215; IFC vol. 1711, pp. 221–224. Kinawley: James G. Delaney,

collector, IFC vol. 1480, pp. 444–450. Killesher: Gailey, *Irish Folk Drama*, pp. 53–58. Florencecourt: Mary Rogers, "Tromogagh Mummers' Play, County Fermanagh," *Ulster Folklife*, 13 (1967), pp. 81–84; the same text is in her *Prospect of Erne: A Study of the Islands and Shores of Lough Erne Co. Fermanagh* (Enniskillen: Watergate Press, 1971), pp. 239–244.

6. Gailey, *Irish Folk Drama*, pp. 80–84; Kevin Danaher, *The Year in Ireland* (Cork: Mercier Press, 1972), pp. 243–258. Danaher provides several interesting early accounts; another good one can be found in W. R. LeFanu, *Seventy Years of Irish Life* (New York: Macmillan, 1894), pp. 113–114. In his folkloristically wonderful book, *A Lad of the O'Friels* (New York: Devin-Adair, 1945), chapter XV, Seumas MacManus amusingly describes the diffusion of the wren hunting custom to an area north of its usual region.

7. Fermanagh Mummings: Belcoo: Alex Helm and E. C. Cawte, *Six Mummers' Acts* (Ibstock, Leicestershire: Guizer Press, 1968), pp. 30–35. Derrygonnelly: Robert Harbinson, *Song of Erne* (London: Faber and Faber, 1960), pp. 199–204; Michael J. Murphy in IFC vol. 1711, pp. 270–271, reports a bit of the play from the same area. Garvary: Gailey, *Christmas Rhymers and Mummers in Ireland*, pp. 35–39.

PERFORMANCE

1. See: Kandinsky and Marc, *The Blaue Reiter Almanac*, pp. 65, 87–89, 150.

2. A laconic American statement can be found in Marvin Harris, *The Rise of Anthropological Theory: A History of Theories of Culture* (New York: Thomas Y. Crowell, 1971), pp. 163–164. A lovely French statement can be found in Claude Lévi-Strauss (John Russell, trans.), *Tristes Tropiques* (New York: Atheneum, 1970), part IX. The current anthropological angst is well presented in Dell Hymes' Introduction to his *Reinventing Anthropology* (New York: Vintage Books, 1974).

3. The particular performance I have in mind took place on New Year's Day Eve, 1890, and was comically versified by James Lumsden in *Sheep-Head and Trotters, Being Savoury Selections,*

Poetic and Prosaic, from the Bulky Literary Remains of Samuel Mucklebackit and Thomas Pintail, Late Parnassian Hill and Arable Farmers in Lothian (Haddington: William Sinclair, 1892), pp. 43–49. The Scots' Hogmanay traditions, including a Goloshan play (pp. 82–86), are nicely described in F. Marian McNeill, *The Silver Bough*, III (Glasgow: William MacLellan, 1961), chapters VIII–XI.

4. Thomas Hardy's deservedly famous description of a mumming of the 1840–1850 period appears in *The Return of the Native* (first published 1878), Book 2, Parts 4 (in which making the costumes is described), 5, and 6.

5. Reminiscing about the customs of his youth in County Armagh, T. G. F. Paterson writes, " . . . the Christmas Rhymers were perhaps the greatest thrill of my boyhood days—the first time I saw Devil Doubt I was greatly alarmed when he recited, 'Money I want and money I crave, if ye don't give me money, I'll sweep ye all till yer grave.' I had none, but, fortunately mother had the 'wherewithal' to save my brothers and me from so dreadful a fate . . . . " See: *Country Cracks: Old Tales from the County of Armagh* (Dundalk: W. Tempest, Dundalgan Press, 1945), p. 14.

6. Interestingly, Alan Gailey in "The Rhymers of South-East Antrim," p. 26, notes that Hector is a Scottish mumming character unknown in Ulster.

7. In *Irish Minstrels and Musicians* (Chicago: Regan Publishing House, 1913), p. 125, Captain Francis O'Neill gives a brief account of mumming and the melody of "The Mummers' March" used in Wexford. There was no special mumming tune in Ballymenone.

8. I heard "Kevin Barry" often in 1972, mostly in bars frequented by Catholic men, but its place as the favorite ballad had been taken by "Sean South of Garryowen," a commemorative account of an I.R.A. raid on the Brookeborough, County Fermanagh, R.U.C. station, New Year's Day, 1957. Folksong collections that might be expected to include "Kevin Barry" and "Sean South" often do not. Patrick Galvin's *Irish Songs of Resistance* (New York: Folklore Press, n.d., c. 1960) has a "Kevin Barry," pp. 67–68, but it is not the song usually sung. Representative texts of the usual "Kevin Barry" can be found in Colm O Lochlainn, *Irish Street Ballads* (New York: Corinth, 1960), pp. 98–99, and Daniel

O'Keeffe, *The First Book of Irish Ballads* (Cork: Mercier Press, 1965), p. 103. Recordings: Liam, Tom, and Patrick Clancy and Tommy Makem, *The Rising of the Moon: Irish Songs of Rebellion* (Tradition: TLP 1006), B:2; Dominic Behan, *Songs of the Irish Republican Army* (Riverside: RLP 12–820), A:4. A very informative pamphlet, Sean Cronin, *The Story of Kevin Barry* (Cork: National Publications Committee, 1971), recounts Barry's life and includes several songs about him. The usual ballad is at pp. 41–42 where it says the song was written by an Irishman living in Glasgow and that it was available on broadside at the time of Barry's execution.

9. Harbinson, *Song of Erne*, pp. 192–193, also 226.

10. Yeats, *The Autobiography*, pp. 7, 29, 319.

11. William Morris, *A Dream of John Ball* (Portland, Maine: Thomas B. Mosher, 1902, first published 1888), p. 19. Despite the thousands of published Irish song and tale texts, there are nearly no published descriptions of the performance of songs and tales. In *Malachi Horan Remembers* (Dublin: M. H. Gill, 1943), George A. Little gives a song as sung, complete with characteristic audience commentary and encouragement (pp. 40–42). The truest data on Irish performance is to be found in fiction, and the best fictional presentation I have found is in the fabulous, hilarious *At Swim-Two-Birds* (London: MacGibbon and Kee, 1966, first published 1939) by Flann O'Brien (Brian O'Nolan). Particularly worthy of notice are Shanahan's reminiscence (pp. 74–82) with the frequent comments of his listeners, the good-manning Casey gets after his poem (p. 173), and Connors' joke with Fogarty's response (pp. 194–195).

12. See Herbert Halpert and G. M. Story, eds., *Christmas Mumming in Newfoundland: Essays in Anthropology, Folklore, and History* (Toronto: University of Toronto Press for Memorial University of Newfoundland, 1969). In at least one area of Ireland people calling themselves mummers have recently stopped performing the play, though they continue to go from house to house at Christmas; they are uncostumed and their goal is music-making. See: Seán Corcoran, "A Mummers' Play from County Louth," *Ceol*, IV:1 (January 1972), pp. 11–16, particularly p. 15.

13. Patrick Kavanagh, *The Green Fool* (London: Martin Brian and O'Keeffe, 1971, first published 1938), pp. 186–192. His

account does not include any of the rhymes, but his poem "The Christmas Mummers," *Collected Poems* (London: MacGibbon and Kee, 1964), pp. 111–114, shows that the play he performed in was well within the Ulster tradition as well as displaying Kavanagh's fine, angry art. In a letter to me (June 9, 1975), the poet's brother, Peter Kavanagh, himself a fine writer and astute observer of Irish culture, writes: "Very interesting about the mummers. I recall them well when I was a child, the excitement and fear as they entered the house near Halloween. 'Room, room, me gallant boys,/ And give us room to rhyme. . . .' I suppose you have got all the variations. I forget. That part of the country was very rich in lore until recently."

MEANING

1. See Caoimhín Ó Danachair, "The Quarter Days in Irish Tradition," *Arv,* 15 (1959), pp. 47–55; John C. Messenger, *Inis Beag: Isle of Ireland*, Case Studies in Cultural Anthropology (New York: Holt, Rinehart and Winston, 1969), pp. 102–106.

2. For St. Brighid's Day crosses, see: T. G. F. Paterson, "Brigid's Crosses in County Armagh," *Ulster Journal of Archaeology*, 3rd Series, 8 (1945), pp. 43–48, and John C. O'Sullivan, "St. Brigid's Crosses," *Folk Life*, 11 (1973), pp. 60–81.

3. At the end of the period of the last mummers, a survey was conducted of selected sections of Ulster. Our area was one of them; it is in Area 2 of County Fermanagh, described in chapter III of John Mogey's *Rural Life in Northern Ireland* (London: Oxford University Press, 1947). In Fermanagh, Mogey reports that four percent of the houses have running water and six percent have electricity. In Area 2, he found two houses with running water, none with electric lights (pp. 36–37). Things have changed in the three decades since Mogey's good study, but most houses still lack water and electricity, and the area's relative economic position remains as he described it. The land is wet, the soil thin, the people poor.

4. The life-cycle explanation is put forth in Margaret Dean-Smith, "The Life-Cycle Play or Folk Play: Some Conclusions Following the Examination of the Ordish Papers and Other Sources," *Folklore*, 69 (December 1958), pp. 237–253. Frazer offers

comments relevant to mumming at many points of *The Golden Bough*, but his main arguments are to be found in vol. II, chapter X, and vol. IV, chapter VIII of the third edition. In order to take a modern look at an idea like that of the connection between mumming and the new year we will need to forget the negative notion of irrational survival and think of the drama as metaphorically moving its participants, rather than magically moving their environment. See: Alan Dundes, "The Devolutionary Premise in Folklore Theory," *Journal of the Folklore Institute*, VI:1 (June 1969), pp. 5–19, and James Fernandez, "The Mission of Metaphor in Expressive Culture," *Current Anthropology*, 15:2 (June 1974), pp. 119–145, particularly pp. 124–129.

5. Chambers linked Devil Doubt to the New Year's Day ashes in *The English Folk-Play*, p. 212. Seán Ó Súilleabháin reports the belief about ash removal on New Year's Day in *Irish Folk Custom and Belief*, Irish Life and Culture, XV (Dublin: Cultural Relations Committee of Ireland, n.d., c. 1970), p. 61. In *The Year in Ireland*, p. 258, Danaher comments on the relative unimportance of New Year's Day in Ireland.

6. A lyrically sad description of south Ulster rural life awaits you in Patrick Kavanagh's poem of 1942, "The Great Hunger": *Collected Poems*, pp. 34–55. In a 1960 radio broadcast, included in Peter Kavanagh, ed., *November Haggard: Uncollected Prose and Verse of Patrick Kavanagh* (New York: Peter Kavanagh Hand Press, 1971), pp. 15–16, he said his long poem was too grim and one-sided. It is. But it is a valuable record, a haunting record of the hollow, bitter side of life in areas like southern Fermanagh. It is mumming's opposite—like mumming, true but partial.

7. In Theodora Fitzgibbon's *A Taste of Ireland: Irish Traditional Food* (London: Pan Books, 1968), p. 12, there is a recipe for boxty quite similar to that used in Fermanagh.

8. The dynamic of the opening of the second act of Samual Beckett's *Waiting for Godot* (New York: Grove Press, 1954), depends upon speech, silence, and human connection. It starts with Vladimir's endless circular tale. They meet again, Estragon says, "Don't speak to me! Stay with me!" At the bottom of p. 40, they agree man's lot is to die and be forgotten and decide to converse calmly so they won't think, but on the following page comes the silence begetting Vladimir's ejaculation.

9. The first chapters of these two books provide descriptions of Twelfth of July celebrations: Sam Hanna Bell, *Erin's Orange Lily* (London: Dennis Dobson, 1956); Tony Gray, *The Orange Order* (London: The Bodley Head, 1972). The thunderous Lambeg drums that announce the Twelfth and the songs that close it can be heard on Samuel B. Charters, *The Orangemen of Ulster* (Folkways Records: F W 3003).

10. My thinking on gift giving was helped by Marcel Mauss (Ian Cunnison, trans.), *The Gift: Forms and Functions of Exchange in Archaic Societies* (New York: W. W. Norton, 1967, first published 1925).

11. James Joyce, *Finnegans Wake* (New York: Viking, 1958, first published 1939), p. 467.

12. In Ireland the egg tree was generally a part of the May Day celebration (Danaher, *The Year in Ireland*, pp. 75–78, 90–95), but P Flanagan's account of an egg bush on Easter is not unique for Ireland or Europe; see Venetia Newall's fine book *An Egg at Easter: A Folklore Study* (Bloomington: Indiana University Press, 1971), pp. 310–312.

13. How different the meaning of mumming is when its actors are little boys and girls rather than mature bachelors. This is the case in the mumming Lynn Doyle reports from the County of Down in his rich book, *An Ulster Childhood* (London: Duckworth, 1927, first published 1921), pp. 130–142.

14. Alan Gailey, "Straw Costume in Irish Folk Customs," *Folk Life*, 6 (1968), pp. 83–84.

15. Quoted from Alexander McConnell's notebooks in the Ulster Folk Museum archive, p. 44.

16. For a few samples from a very rich literature: On bonfires: Máire MacNeill, *The Festival of Lughnasa: A Study of the Survival of the Celtic Festival of the Beginning of Harvest* (London: Oxford University Press, 1962), pp. 205, 230, 242; Ronald H. Buchanan, "Calendar Customs: Part I. New Year's Day to Michaelmas," *Ulster Folklife*, 8 (1962), pp. 22–24; Ronald H. Buchanan, "Calendar Customs: Part 2. Harvest to Christmas," *Ulster Folklife*, 9 (1963), p. 65; Sheila St. Clair, *Folklore of the Ulster People* (Cork: Mercier Press, 1971), pp. 38–41; Danaher, *The Year in Ireland*, pp. 95–96, 209. On processions: Buchanan, "Calendar Customs: Part I," p. 20; "Part 2," p. 75; Gailey, "Straw Costume

in Irish Folk Customs," pp. 91–92; Gailey, *Irish Folk Drama*, pp. 85–86; Danaher, *The Year in Ireland*, pp. 24–37, 78–79, 210–214, 243–258; Richard Hilliard, "Biddies and Straw Boys," *Ulster Folklife*, 8 (1962), pp. 100–102. On wake wrestlers: Seán Ó Súilleabháin, *Irish Wake Amusements* (Cork: Mercier Press, 1967), p. 40.

17. The painter Ad Rinehardt offers a good statement in "Writings" in Gregory Battcock, ed., *The New Art: A Critical Anthology* (New York: E. P. Dutton, 1966), pp. 199–209: "The next revolution [in Art] will see the return . . . to the folk-places and lower-depths where it all came from in the first place" (p. 204). "Less in art is not less. More in art is not more" (p. 207).

18. The assumption in my search for meaning is that there is a logic in the unconscious. Freud, Yeats, Faulkner, Joyce, and particularly Claude Lévi-Strauss have convinced me that at least some of this logic can be exposed through inquiry guided but not inhibited by the idea of pairing and opposition.

FUNCTION

1. See: Chambers, *The English Folk-Play*, p. 105. A recent discussion of this text is Michael J. Preston, "The Revesby Sword Play," *Journal of American Folklore*, 85:335 (January–March 1972), pp. 51–57. Texts cannot carry us deeply into time, but our entrance to the farther past is not completely blocked. In a marvelous painting of 1559, Peter Brueghel depicts the conflict of Carnival and Lent. At the left rear in Carnival's domain, he shows the end of a street drama. It has five characters, including a wild man with a great club (a Beelzebub); two combatants, one of them a king carrying a sword and wearing a long robe; and a masked man in women's clothes. The householder is leaning over a half door, giving the mummers his, apparently monetary, donation. See: Gustav Glück, *Peter Brueghel the Elder* (London: Thames and Hudson, 1958), plate 12, detail 12a.

2. See: Alan Gailey, "A New Year Custom in South-East Ulster," in Walter Escher, Theo Gantner, and Hans Trümpy, eds., *Festschrift Für Robert Wildhaber* (Basel: Schweizerische Gesellschaft für Volkskunde, 1973), pp. 126–136, especially p. 130. The Rathlin Island "Hogmany Meal" collectors are described in Bell,

Erin's Orange Lily, pp. 136–138; see too: John Braidwood, "The Rathlin Rite of the 'Coullin,' " *Ulster Folklife*, 14 (1968), pp. 44–50.

3. Samuel Beckett, *Molloy* (London: Calder and Boyars, 1960, first published 1950), p. 41.

4. In its heyday, functionalism was formulated in several different ways. Within modern folklore it is most usefully conceived as an act's consequences, whether foreseeable or not, whether encouraging social cohesion or not. Social functionalism's classic statement is A. R. Radcliffe-Brown, "On the Concept of Function in Social Science," *American Anthropologist*, 37 (July–September 1935), pp. 394–402. An important critique and reformulation is Robert K. Merton's "Manifest and Latent Functions" in *On Theoretical Sociology: Five Essays, Old and New* (New York: Free Press, 1967), pp. 73–138.

5. Gailey, *Irish Folk Drama*, p. 10.

6. The connection between Stephen and the martyr comes in *A Portrait of the Artist as a Young Man* (New York: Viking, 1956, first published 1916), p. 159. The Nighttown section of *Ulysses* (1934) is pp. 422–593. Its anticipation is pp. 212–215.

7. Richard Ellmann's superb biography of Joyce excitingly reveals the autobiographical richness in *Ulysses*. Stephen is Joyce, but so is Bloom. Bloom is Jewish, and Joyce was fascinated with the comparable marginality of Jews and Irishmen. He thought, it seems, that Jews embodied the loving, gentle side of the Irish. Private Carr knocks Stephen down in Nighttown. While writing *Ulysses,* Joyce was verbally assaulted by a Private Carr with whom he became engaged in a lawsuit. That Carr was an actor and an official English representative. Joyce's encounter with him increased Joyce's anger at England and affection for Ireland. During the period of *Ulysses,* Joyce's bitterness against Ireland turned into love—love even for the peasants and the misty, Celtic west. The book describes June 16, 1904, Bloomsday. In 1904, Joyce began work on the book that would become *A Portrait*: he was on his way to artistic maturity. On June 16 of that year, Joyce fell in love with Nora Barnacle who brought him the feminine stability he lost in his mother's death, and who he said, "made me a man." The book records the Bloom in Joyce, the feminine and mature in him, becoming father to the Stephen in him; it records

the victory of forces for psychic unity. See: Ellmann's *James Joyce* (New York: Oxford University Press, 1972, first published 1959), pp. 161–167, 238–239, 252–263, 268, 276, 289, 303, 309, 336, 369, 381–390, 436–441, 454–467, 471, 520–521, 715.

8. Toward an entry for mumming in a *Finnegans Wake* concordance: The Great Days and death: 308 ("youlldied greedings"), 455, 472, 556. Battles: 80–82, 338–341 (338: "gobrawl"), 361 (Patrick and the "bester of the boyne"; also Arthur, maker of Guinness stout, and the British king who lives on after death), 499–501. Mumming and politics: 48, 82 ("Capn," "Billi," Christmas, death and revival), 114–115 (Boyne), 219, 310 (South vs. North), 473 (marching phoenix: "whimsicalissimo"), 499–501 (Cromwellian battle ends with bonfires, murmuring). Mumming with mother pun: 373, 396, 428. Mumming with sex: 535 (H. C. E. is Haveth Childers Everywhere), 569 ("Mumm me moe mummers!"; "genitalmen from Veruno"—Bruno and mummery). "Mumtiplay": 283. Mummers and crime: 356. Mumming characters: Wrenboys' rhyme: 44, 45, 348, 363 ("...keen of old bards"), 376, 430, 431, 504; Beelzebub: 64, 239, 310, 580; Myles the Slasher: 99, 283; George: 327 ("munin"), 335 ("Bullyclubber"); Doctor: 254 ("murmury"); Big Head: 320. The dense section pp. 219–259 opens and closes "mum" and refers to the Turk.

9. James L. Peacock has given us a fine study of ludruk in *Rites of Modernization: Symbolic and Social Aspects of Indonesian Proletarian Drama* (Chicago: University of Chicago Press, 1968).

10. This is the point at which my continual debt to Kenneth Burke's genius is most apparent. His most closely relevant essay is chapter 5 of Part III of *Language as Symbolic Action* (Berkeley and Los Angeles: University of California Press, 1968), but it was Part I of that book and especially his *A Grammar of Motives* (Berkeley and Los Angeles: University of California Press, 1969, first published 1945), that inspired me most.

11. See: Carroll Edward Mace, *Two Spanish-Quiché Dance Dramas of Rabinal*, Studies in Romance Languages and Literature, 3 (New Orleans: Tulane University, 1970).

12. Some problems of revival are considered in Alex Helm, "In Comes I, St. George," *Folklore*, 76 (Summer 1965), pp. 118–136, especially pp. 126–132.

13. Mumming chapbooks, including a famous one printed in

Belfast, are described in: Alex Helm, *The Chapbook Mummers'
Plays: A Study of the Printed Versions of the North-West of
England* (Ibstock, Leicestershire: Guizer Press, 1969); Alan
Gailey, "A Missing Belfast Chapbook: The Christmas Rime, or the
Mummers' Own Book," *Irish Booklore*, 2:1 (Spring 1972), pp.
54–58; and Alan Gailey, "Chapbook Influences on Irish Mum-
mers' Plays," *Folklore*, 85 (Spring 1974), pp. 1–22.

14. The local impact of the events of the 1900–1925 period is
well described in Peadar Livingstone's *The Fermanagh Story: A
Documented History of the County Fermanagh from the Earliest
Times to the Present Day* (Enniskillen: Cumann Seanchais
Chlochair, 1969), chapters 22–26.

15. Michael J. Murphy's description of mumming appears in
his excellent book, *At Slieve Gullion's Foot* (Dundalk: W. Tempest, Dundalgan Press, 1945), pp. 97–101. Murphy's sensitive writings are good introductions to country life in south Ulster; see
also: *Mountain Year* (Dublin: The Dolmen Press, 1964); and
Tyrone Folk Quest (Belfast: Blackstaff Press, 1973). The latter
book engagingly describes his work as one of the Irish Folklore
Commission's fulltime collectors.

16. Cawte, Helm and Peacock point out the distributional
similarity of mumming and openfield villages in *English Ritual
Drama*, pp. 32–33, 35. The exceptions to the failure of mumming
in the New World are few. The tradition has continued in the
Caribbean, nurtured surely by an Afro-American tendency to cooperative forms of art and labor. Herbert Halpert's "A Typology
of Mumming" in the book *Christmas Mumming in Newfoundland*,
which he co-edited with G. M. Story, sets out the relationship of
the Newfoundland mummings to those in Britain and other places
in North America. The excellent papers in that volume by Fire-
stone, Chiaramonte, Szwed (in particular), Ben-Dor and Faris
suggest a relationship between mumming and society like that
in Fermanagh. Of the three Newfoundland texts, all dating from
1900 or earlier, two are apparently Irish in origin (pp. 144–207).
Mumming was known in nineteenth century Philadelphia, where
rather than dying out it became one of the elements incorporated
into a grand parade as described by Charles E. Welch in *Oh! Dem
Golden Slippers* (New York: Thomas Nelson, 1970). The com-

munal traditions that were not forgotten in America were made formal and gigantic.

17. Though Ireland is generally considered a place of independent farms, recent scholarship has emphasized the importance of housing clusters and cooperative land use; see: E. Estyn Evans, *The Personality of Ireland: Habitat, Heritage, and History* (Cambridge: Cambridge University Press, 1973), pp. 52–62; R. H. Buchanan, "Rural Settlement in Ireland," in Nicholas Stephens and Robin E. Glasscock, eds., *Irish Geographical Studies in Honour of E. Estyn Evans* (Belfast: Department of Geography, The Queen's University, 1970), pp. 146–161, especially 152–154; Kevin Danaher, *The Pleasant Land of Ireland* (Cork: Mercier Press, 1970), pp. 14–20; F. H. A. Aalen and Hugh Brody, *Gola: The Life and Last Days of an Island Community* (Cork: Mercier Press, 1969), pp. 33–41. The Ballymenone landscape lies conceptually equidistant from the agricultural poles represented by the individualized farmstead of rural nineteenth century America and the village of the late medieval English Midlands. Excellent anthropological work in County Clare distinguished three degrees of cooperation in Irish farm work: family work, cooring, and the meitheal; see: Conrad M. Arensberg and Solon T. Kimball, *Family and Community in Ireland* (Cambridge: Harvard University Press, 1968, first published 1940), pp. 59–75, 254–257. In Clare and Fermanagh most work is carried on by the farm's family, although cooperative trading and combining are also frequent. The term "coor" is known in Ballymenone, though "joining" is the usual word, and unlike Clare, cooring is not restricted to extended family groups. For more on cooperative work, see: Robin Morton, *Come Day, Go Day, God Send Sunday: The Songs and Life Story, Told in His Own Words, of John Maguire, Traditional Singer and Farmer from Co. Fermanagh* (London: Routledge and Kegan Paul, 1973), pp. 31 ("mechal"), 93–94 ("joins"); E. Estyn Evans, *Irish Folk Ways* (New York: Devin-Adair, 1957), pp. 20–26, 142; Conrad Arensberg, *The Irish Countryman: An Anthropological Study* (Garden City: Natural History Press, 1968, first published 1937), pp. 68–75, 121–123; Hugh Brody, *Inishkillane: Change and Decline in the West of Ireland* (New York: Schocken Books, 1974), pp. 26–27, 131–134.

18. My references are to works by Samuel Beckett who, better than any social scientist, has limned our image: *The Lost Ones* (New York: Grove Press, 1972); *Malone Dies* (New York: Grove Press, 1956); *Happy Days* (New York: Grove Press, 1961); *Waiting for Godot.*

Index

Achebe, Chinua, 54
agriculture (tools, practice, economy), xiv–xv, 4, 7, 12, 18, 20–21, 35, 101, 110, 113–114, 119, 121–123, 126, 139–140, 146–147, 154–155, 157–159, 160–161, 187
Antrim (county in Ireland), 125
architecture, xiv–xv, 4–5, 7–8, 15, 60, 64, 94, 102, 139. *See also* hearth
Armagh (county in Ireland), 137
Armstrong, Robert Plant, 173
Arney River, xiii, 12–13, 114, 159
Artaud, Antonin, 65–66

Ballymenone (Fermanagh), xiv, xviii, 34, 74, 136
Barry, Kevin, 87–88, 130
Bauhaus, 127
Beckett, Samuel, 66, 104–106, 127, 133, 140, 142, 181
Belcoo (Fermanagh), 74–75
Belfast, 8, 12, 88, 149
belief, 97, 103, 109–115. *See also* luck
Bellanaleck (Fermanagh), xiii, 4, 34, 70, 145–146
Belsnickels, 125
Boho (Fermanagh), 74
bonfires, 100–102, 107, 110–111, 119, 140
Boyle, Michael, xviii, 36, 38–49, 57, 59, 66, 72, 74–75, 78–79, 82–83, 85, 127, 142, 145–146, 148, 150, 157, 175
Brecht, Bertolt, 65
Brendel, John B., 125
Broc's Moon, 114

calendar, 95–96: Great Days, Set Times, 21, 96–98, 103–121. *See also* Christmas; Doon Sunday; Easter; Hallowe'en; Harvest Home; Lammas; May Day; Midsummer; Midwinter; New Year's Day; Palm Sunday; quarter days; St. Bri-

ghid's Day; St. Patrick's Day; St. Stephen's Day; Twelfth Night; Twelfth of July
Cassidy, Peter, 136
Cavan (county in Ireland), 73–74
ceili, 5, 13, 18–19, 49, 60, 88, 92, 102, 104–107, 110, 140, 147–148, 154
Chambers, E. K., 55
chapbooks, 135
Christmas, 12, 21–22, 26, 48, 49, 59–60, 78, 90, 97–100, 102, 106–107, 110, 112, 114, 118–119, 125, 137, 140, 146. *See also* Midwinter
Christmas candle, 102
clothing, 21, 36, 161
Coleman, Michael, 20
community (face-to-face social organization), xii–xiii, 18–19, 49, 110–111, 124–129, 133–140, 142, 147
cookery (food, preparation, and meals), 3–5, 11, 12, 20, 105–106, 109 110, 115, 147, 156, 160
Cork, 58
costume (mummers' disguise), 5, 16–17, 23, 25, 29, 39–40, 60, 68, 78–83, 100, 114–115, 118, 123
coullin, 125
Cromwell, Oliver, 16. *See also* mummers
Cutler, Ellen, xv, xviii, 3–10, 16, 21–22, 66, 86, 92, 102, 105, 108, 112, 122–123, 137, 145, 148–151, 157

dance, 8, 17, 33, 44, 84, 87, 92–93, 99, 107, 115–117, 124, 134
Derrygonnelly (Fermanagh), 75
Derrylester (Fermanagh), 34
Derrylin (Fermanagh), xiv, 21, 34, 71
De Valera, Eamon, 136
Donegal (county in Ireland), 69
Doon Sunday, 21, 97, 114
dramatism, 133–134

drink, 4, 26, 79, 99, 105, 107, 133–134, 157–158
Dublin, 13, 74, 88, 130

Easter, 97–98, 107, 109, 111, 113–114, 119
egg tree, 109, 111, 113–114
Enniskillen (Fermanagh), xii, 12, 22, 29, 34, 39, 89, 108, 142, 145, 150
entertainment, 36, 48, 92–93, 100–101, 104–110, 112, 117, 121, 125, 131–133

fairies, xv, 7, 27, 101–102, 156–157
Farmer, Charlie, 148
Fermanagh (county in Ireland), xii–xiv, 73–74
Flanagan, Joseph, xviii, 20–38, 66, 78, 105, 107–108, 113, 122, 127, 137, 145–149
Flanagan, Peter, xviii–xix, 20–38, 45, 57, 66, 69–74, 78–80, 83–86, 88, 91–93, 98–105, 107–109, 112–114, 116–118, 122–123, 128–129, 132–133, 136–139, 142, 145–149, 151
Flanagan, Phil, 45, 78
Florencecourt (Fermanagh), 74
folklore, as a discipline, xvi–xvii, 22, 55–57, 73, 85, 122, 132, 135–136. See also genres
Ford of Biscuits, Arney River, 13
Frazer, Sir James, 56, 103, 171
Freud, Sigmund, 117
functionalism, 121, 125–129, 134–137, 184
furniture, 3–4, 11, 86–87, 119, 154–156

Gailey, Alan, xi, 129
Galway (county in Ireland), 55
Garvary (Fermanagh), 75
genres, domains of folkloristic concern. See agriculture; architecture; belief; calendar; conversation (see ceili); clothing; community; cookery; dance; drama (see mumming); drink; furniture; music; proverb; riddle; song; tale; toasts; wakes; weddings; witchcraft
George V, 4–5, 133. See also mummers
Gregory, Lady Augusta, 54–55

Hallowe'en (Hallow Eve), 97, 105–107, 114–116, 118–119
Hardy, Thomas, 79
Harvest Home, 114

hearth, 3, 10–11, 13, 28, 94, 104–105, 148
Hogmanay men, 69–70, 77–78
holidays. See calendar

Inishmore (Fermanagh), xiv, 24, 34, 71
Irish Folklore Commission, 73–74

Joyce, James, 54, 59, 63–66, 105, 130–134, 173–174, 184–185

Kandinsky, Wassily, 59, 63–65, 76, 174
Kavanagh, Patrick, 92, 179–181
Killesher (Fermanagh), 74
Kinawley (Fermanagh), xiv, 25, 34, 71, 74, 108, 148
Klee, Paul, 63, 174
Knockninny (Fermanagh), xiv, 74

Lammas, 97, 119
Lévi-Strauss, Claude, 62–63, 65–66, 173–174
Lisnaskea (Fermanagh), 74
Lough Erne, xii–xiv, 12, 24, 34, 71, 74–75, 155, 158
Love, Tommy, 122, 146
luck, 9, 97, 103, 109–114, 117, 121–122, 133–134
Lunny, Johnny, 45
Lunny, Tommy, 137

McBrien, Jemmy, 45, 78
McBrien, John, 36, 45, 78, 116, 136
McBrien, Oney, 148
McBrien, Paddy, 18, 36, 45, 78, 146
McConnell, Alexander, 74
McGiveney, Hugh, 148
Mackan (Fermanagh), 13
Maguire, John Joe, 148
Maguire, Mick, 148
May Day, 97, 103, 110–112, 114, 119
Merriam, Alan P., 173
Midsummer (Saint John's Eve, Bonfire Night), 97, 100–103, 107, 110–111, 119
Midwinter (the context for Christmas), 98–100, 102–103, 134
modernism, 62–64, 76, 121
Molly Maguires, 136
Monaghan (county in Ireland), 92
Morris, William, 53–56, 61, 63–64, 90, 170
mummers (mumming characters): Beelzebub, 5–6, 28–31, 40–41, 74, (Billsie Bob), 82, 85, 107, 117, 122–

mummers—*cont.*
124; Big Head (Musician), 8, 17,
26, 33, 40, 44, 72, 82, 85, 87, 92, 107,
123–124; Captain Mummer, 5, 14,
16, 25, 27–28, 32, 40–41, 43, 66, 74,
79, 82, 84–87, 89, 92, 94, 99, 115–116,
123–124, 137, 146; Dan O'Connell,
69; Doctor, 5–6, 16, 32–33, 39, 40,
43–44, 68, 75 (Doctor Bighead),
78 (Doctor Gore), 80, 82, 86–87,
90, 106–107, 110, 119, 123–124, 134;
"followers," the, 84, 93, 127; Goloshan, 77–78; Green Knight, 74;
Hector, 84, 107, 123–124; Jack
Straw, 82–85, 106, 117–118, 123–
124; Johnny Funny, 69; King
James, 129; Lady, 75; Little Devil
Doubt, 16–17, 74–75, 82–86, 103,
118, 123–124; Miss Funny, 17, 33,
40, 44, 69, 78, 80, 82, 83 (Biddy
Funny), 84–85, 88–89, 92, 99, 117,
123–125, 127; Napoléon, 78; Oliver
Cromwell, 14–15, 40, 42, 69, 75, 82,
85, 123–124, 129; Prince Albert, 84;
Prince George, 28–29, 31, 40, 42–
43, 69 (Saint George), 74–75, 78,
82, 85, 123–124, 129, 133, 135
(Saint); Saint Patrick, 15–16, 40–
43, 69, 74, 78, 82, 85, 106, 114, 119,
123–124, 129, 133–134, 146; Tom
Funny, 75; Turkey Champion, 69,
74 (Grand Turk), 84 (Grand),
135; William of Orange, 129
Mummers' Ball, 23, 36, 48, 79, 89, 92,
99, 100–101, 107, 110, 112, 116–117,
124, 127, 129, 134
Mummers' Rule, 25–27, 48, 69, 79,
86, 92, 126, 136
mumming, history and distribution:
xi, 57–58, 68–75, 134–142; England,
xi, 61, 69, 84, 135, 138–139; Greece,
68; Ireland, 69–75, 84, 135–142;
Newfoundland, 90–91; Scotland,
xi, 22, 69–70, 77–78, 135; United
States, 138–139; West Indies, 61
Murphy, Michael J., 74, 137–138, 186
music (instruments, tunes, performance), 8, 13, 17, 20–21, 29, 33, 44,
84, 87, 92, 99, 101, 106–108, 126–
127, 134, 136–137, 148

New Year's Day, 22, 69, 73, 78, 99,
103–104, 125
New York, 29
Nolan, Hugh, xviii, 11–19, 38, 66,
69, 72, 77, 85, 97–99, 102, 108, 112–

113, 122, 129, 136, 138, 146, 148,
150, 175

O'Casey, Sean, 65
Orange Order, xiii, 4, 88, 102, 108
Owens, Hugh Patrick, 18
Owens, James, 45, 48–49, 136, 142

Palm Sunday, 98. *See also* Easter
Pennsylvania, 125
politics (the Troubles), XV, 8–9,
12–13, 16, 34–35, 37, 53, 58, 87–88,
108, 115, 126, 129–137, 149–150
positivism, 56–57, 94–95
proverb, proverbial comparison, 105,
123, 125, 155

quarter days, 96–97
Quigley, Benny, 36, 45, 78
Quigley, Paddy, 36, 45, 78

Rathlin Island, 125
rationalism, 62, 173
Reed, Ola Belle, 60
relativism, 76–77
religion, xiii, xv, 31, 108, 115, 118–
119, 126–130, 135
riddle, 117
romanticism, 53–56, 61–64
Ruskin, John, 61, 64, 172–173

Saint Brighid's Day, 97, 111–112, 119
Saint George, 130. *See also* mummers
Saint Patrick, 101, 118, 130–131. *See
also* mummers
Saint Patrick's Day, 98, 100, 106, 107–
108, 113, 119
Saint Stephen's Day (Boxing Day,
Second Day of Christmas), 22, 48,
70, 74, 98, 131
Shakespeare, William, 75, 121
shamrock, 113
Sinn Fein, 88, 135–136
Sligo (county in Ireland), 53, 63
song (ballad text and performance),
XII, 33, 38, 60, 87–88, 90, 93, 101,
106–108, 121, 126, 129–130, 132,
136, 140, 148, 150, 158
strawboys, 70, 75, 115–117, 133
structuralism, 61–62, 121, 165
survivalism, xi–xii, 55–62, 102–104,
121, 127–128, 134–135

tale (memorat, tall tale and märchen,
text and performance), 27, 31–32,
69–71, 90, 101–102, 104, 106, 127,
138, 175

Index

Tiddy, R. J. E., xvi
toasts, 113
Twelfth Night, 68, 99
Twelfth of July, 97, 102, 108

Ulster Folk Museum, 74

wakes, 119, 132
weddings, 115–117, 119

Wexford (county in Ireland), 69
William of Orange, 4, 13. *See also* mummers
witchcraft, 111
wrenboys, 70, 72–74, 112, 123, 131
Wright, Frank Lloyd, 64

Yeats, William Butler, 53–56, 59, 61, 63, 65, 88, 174–175